How To
BUILD A
CARPORT

the easy way
a step-by-step guide

Penny Swift & Janek Szymanowski

First published in 2013 by PJ's Design Workshop
PO Box 558
Somerset Mall 7137
Somerset West
Western Cape
South Africa
http://pjdesign.pennyswift.com

Text © Penny Swift
Photographs © Janek Szymanowski
Illustrations © Penny Swift and Janek Szymanowski
Design: Janek Szymanowki
Printing and binding, softcover edition: CreateSpace

ISBN softcover 978-0-620-58366-4

CONTENTS

INTRODUCTION

Owing to the limitations of either space or budget, or both, more and more houses are being built without garages. Furthermore, because of escalating building costs, those people who do have garages often convert them to provide room for storage or an extension to their living space. These factors have resulted in a marked increase in the popularity of carports, as they provide an easy alternative to the garage as an area to park your car. The addition of a carport can be a particularly simple, effective and comparatively inexpensive home improvement project.

Tastefully designed and properly constructed, a carport will provide a practical parking place for your car (or caravan, if you have one), add to the aesthetic appeal of your house, and increase the resale value of your property.

This book contains some imaginative ideas and sound advice for homeowners wishing to construct a carport, and deals with all practical considerations related to planning, designing and building a structure to suit your needs. Project plans are offered as examples, together with a checklist of materials required for each job. However, formal building plans will have to be drawn up and submitted to your local authority before construction can begin. No two sets of plans will be quite the same, as the individual property will have to be taken into account and the exact site of the structure indicated.

How To Build A Carport the easy way will be invaluable, not only to the keen home builder, but also to those who want to cost and assess the project in terms of time and work required, quantities of materials needed, and problems which may have to be overcome. Even if you decide to employ somebody else to do the work for you, knowing what is required will enable you to check that the job is being done properly.

ABOVE
Attaching a gutter to a sturdy well-built carport that will add value to the property.

RIGHT
A simple structure designed to shelter cars.

FAR RIGHT
An attractive carport assembled with steel uprights and factory manufactured brackets.

CHAPTER ONE
Planning

Basic Principles

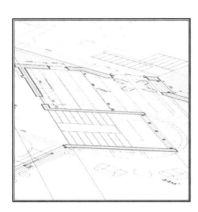

A carport is a permanent structure and a worthwhile investment that warrants proper planning. It should be chosen carefully to blend with the style of your house and garden. Unfortunately structures are often erected quickly and without any thought, resulting in an embarrassing eyesore that does nothing to enhance the property or its neighbourhood.

As most city or regional authorities have zoning ordinances, building codes and regulations that require formal plans before they will give consent for the erection of even the most basic carport, practical outhouses like garden sheds or storerooms may easily be included in the drawings. Clever planning may even provide you with a framework that can be converted to a garage at a later stage (see box, Planning for the future, page 18).

FUNCTION

A major consideration when planning a carport is the function you wish it to fulfil. Do you simply want a structure that says: "Park your car here"? Do you want something to improve the aesthetic appeal of your home? Do you want a solid roof that will offer protection from vertical rain, hail or snow; or do you simply want to keep your vehicle cool in sunny weather?

Once you have established your needs, you will be in a good position to decide what type of structure to build.

A defined area to park your car The simplest carport is little more than a pergola or an attractive framework of some kind. It is usually made from gum poles, although cut-and-planed timber, metal or fiber-cement poles can also be used. It may have no distinct parking surface and no roof, but it effectively provides an acceptable home base for vehicles.

A decorative feature A carport structure may do nothing more than improve the aesthetic appeal of your property. Decorative structures are frequently erected over an attractive paved area to frame the entrance to a property. While its practical benefits may be negligible, a successful decorative carport will improve the visual impact of a house.

A shelter from the elements A carport that protects a vehicle from the elements will have some kind of protective covering that forms a roof. Practicality is the key word here, as the function of the carport will be to protect your car from rain, sun, hail or snow. A variety of coverings, that fulfil different functions, are discussed in detail in Roofing (see pages 37 to 40). Local climate and individual needs will dictate the materials used for any type of shelter.

CHOOSING THE SITE

There is often one obvious site for a carport - in front of or alongside the garage, or adjacent to the front entrance of the house - but this is not always the case. If there is more than one option, consider the advantages and disadvantages of each. Look for any drop kerbs that might already be in place otherwise that must be installed, and remember, ideally, the materials of your carport and driveway paring surfaces should match.

There must, of course, be enough room to park one or more cars, with space to open car doors comfortably. If you want to locate the structure next to the house, make sure you aren't going to block to much light from existing

ABOVE
Planning on paper is essential to completing a project successfully, even if formal plans are not required by the local authority.

RIGHT
More than adequate protection is provided by this glass fiber carport roof, making it perfectly functional.

PREVIOUS PAGE
A vine-covered wooden structure above the brick paved driveway gives shelter from the sun under this charming carport.

windows. If there are trees nearby, ascertain whether they will affect the structure. Will any trees have to be felled before building begins, and, if not, will overhanging branches affect or endanger the structure once it is complete?

Inspect the ground on which you plan to build. Is it sound, or will additional foundations be necessary? If the land slopes, are retaining walls required? Do you have to remove soil; or must you bring in fill to help level the site?

You should also consider access to the carport, as you may find it necessary to incorporate a driveway in your planning if the carport is sited away from the street.

Minimum space requirements The most obvious prerequisite for a carport is sufficient ground on which to build. A single carport should be no smaller than 3 m x 5.5 m (9.8 ft x 18 ft) while a double carport should be at least 5.5 m x 5.5 m (18 ft x 18 ft). However, if space permits, it is advisable to increase these sizes to 3 m x 6 m (9.8 ft x 19.6 ft) and 6 m x 6 m (19.6 ft x 19.6 ft) for additional protection. Personal requirements may dictate an even bigger space.

The recommended height for a carport is 2,4 m (7.9 ft) from finished floor to underside of roof covering or crossbeams, though it might be wise to increase this slightly if the structure is likely to have to accommodate a boat, caravan or roof racks. No structure should be less than 2,1 m (6.9 ft) high.

Accessibility to dwelling A practical consideration when choosing the site for your carport is accessibility to your front (or back) door. A carport built any distance from the house may give vehicles protection on rainy days, but it certainly won't keep the occupants dry as they dash for the front door. If you live in a high-rainfall area, it may be worth considering the incorporation of a covered walkway from the carport to the house. This may simply mean extending the roof covering from carport to front door; or it may require the erection of an additional structure.

DESIGN & STYLE

Your final consideration when planning your carport will be an aesthetic one. In order for your carport to have a pleasing visual effect, it is essential that it be designed to fit in with the style of the other buildings on your premises. If you have a quaint Victorian home and are planning to site the carport beside it, a facebrick structure would be inappropriate. Similarly, a rustic gum-pole structure would look wrong beside a clean-lined, modern home. Once it is built, you don't want your carport to look as though it was an ill-conceived afterthought.

BELOW LEFT
Maximum use of minimal space; all the available area has been used to provide a carport which will protect the car.

BELOW RIGHT
The value of this carport is in the added aesthetic appeal it gives to the property. There is nothing functional about it.

BOTTOM LEFT
This carport was built as an extension to the house, and provides sheltered access from the house to the car.

BOTTOM RIGHT
This simple structure, made of fiber-cement piping, affords no protection, merely demarcating the area in which the car should be parked.

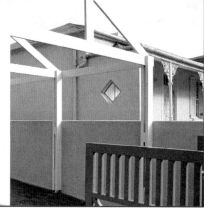

Carport Ideas

Before you decide exactly what you're going to build, consider your options. Drive around and get ideas from other people's carports, and study the plans on pages 55-61. Remember that you should let your carport blend with your home and garden, matching it with existing styles, or picking up distinctive features - perhaps by using similar materials. It is also a good idea to try to make your carport work for you in other ways than just housing your car. Perhaps you could make it double as a storage space, or a play area for children.

ABOVE
An all-in-one double carport and walkway to the front door is achieved by extending the roof covering of a carport to protect people on a rainy day.

ABOVE RIGHT
This structure has been bolted onto the walls of the house, above both the garage and front door, thereby creating a covered walkway.

CENTER RIGHT
This simple timber structure serves both as a carport and a covered utility area for bins.

BOTTOM RIGHT
The opening in the roof of this carport allows the growth of lush tropical plants in an effective planter, and lets light into what would otherwise be a fairly dark interior. Clever use has been made of a perfect alcove for parking the car, and the roof has simply been extended over three conveniently consructed walls.

TOP
Although it is of little practical value, this carport successfully captures and enhances the Spanish feel of the house.

ABOVE LEFT
A well-planned carport may give protection to boats, sailboards and motor vehicles. Care should be taken to ensure that boats and/or boards are thoroughly secured to prevent them coming loose and damaging the vehicles parked beneath.

ABOVE RIGHT
This attractive carport is bolted to the front wall of the house. Provided it is protected from the street, a well-covered carport like this can easily double as a play area for children in rainy weather.

LEFT
A substantial double carport built alongside the house stretches from an outside wall to four solid-brick pillars which create an almost continuous wall and provide a considerable amount of protection along the side.

BOTTOM LEFT
An innovative, triple gum-pole carport, with varying roof heights, gives added versatility to the standard carport structure. Cars with stacked roof racks, or even caravans, can park in the section on the left.

ROLE OF THE PROFESSIONAL

As properly drawn plans often have to be submitted for carport constructions, you are likely to require the services of at least one professional person - somebody who knows how to do the drawings correctly.

Requirements vary in different countries, and indeed in different parts of many countries. Whatever the requirements are, you will need to familiarize yourself with the relevant laws, codes and regulations.

These are professionals who will be able to help you.

Architects You may feel that, as this is simply a carport, you don't need to spend extra money on design. However, the assistance of an architect or building designer can be invaluable at the planning stage, especially if you want to ensure that the design of your new carport blends with the house and adds value to your property. Most architects charge an hourly fee for consultations, and will get as involved in the project as you want.

Draughtsperson Many registered draughtsmen (and women) operate on a freelance basis and will undertake the drawing and submission of all plans for you. You will usually have to supply all specifications and information regarding the siting of the structure, and materials required.

Building contractors Builders will undertake the entire project for you, from submission of plans (if required) through ordering of materials to building. Before signing a contract, ask to see other carports they have built. If you are on a tight budget is sometimes advisable to organise and supply the materials yourself to avoid additional costs.

Specialist carport companies These companies are specialists in erecting carports, though they seldom undertake the provision of a parking slab or surface. Most specialise in one type of carport structure which may or may not suit the style of your house, so ask to see examples of their designs.

Subcontractors A compromise between employing a builder and doing the job yourself is to hire specialist artisans to help you. These can be either hired by the hour, or paid a previously negotiated fee for the entire job. You will have to order in materials and supervise the work yourself and must therefore know something about the building operations in progress.

Special consultants Engineers and other specialists may sometimes provide a valuable service if the site is a tricky one. Clay soil, huge rocks and sloping ground can cause problems if proper precautions are not taken at the outset.

ABOVE
An architect using up-to-date Computer Aided Design (CAD) applications can design precise and aesthetically pleasing plans for your carport. He can then print them onto paper sizes that will suit the requirements of your local authority.

BUILDING CODES & REGULATIONS

Building codes, zoning ordinances and various regulations that relate to construction will all affect your project. While these will vary depending where you live, they all have the same basic motivation in terms of ensuring that structures are safe and properly built.

In addion to building codes, there are national standards in all countries. Here are some examples:

United States of America In the USA the American National Standards Institute (ANSI) is the primary body that controls standards, though there are other specialist bodies that are involved with setting standards. For example the American Wood Council developed the National Design Specification for Wood Construction that was approved by ANSI, while the American Society of Mechanical Engineers (ASME) and the American Welding Society (AWS) developed standards for welding (which will, of course, apply to metal carport structures).

United Kingdom and Europe In the UK and Europe there are Eurocodes that are published as individual European Standards (EN), each covering different types of structural design, timber, steel, masonry, concrete and so on, as well as a wide range of products and services in other industries. These are maintained and updated by the European Committee for Standardization (CEN).

Australia The Australian Building Codes Board (ABCB) addresses vast and varied issues relating to construction, including sustainability and design. In addition, the ABCB has produced and maintains a set of codes for the design and construction of buildings and other structures in Australia. These are reviewed and amended annually.

South Africa The South African Bureau of Standards (SABS) is responsible for standardizing and maintaining the quality of all products in the country. Standards SA, a section within the SABS, is responsible for writing the standards - known as South African National Standards or SANS - for all the different industries, including construction. The National Building Regulations and Building Standards Act is the law that outlines the basics, while a group of standards (SANS 10400) details what designers, builders, manufacturers and developers need to do to ensure that the legislation is complied with.

There are also a large number of international standards developed by the Swiss-based International Organization for Standardisation (ISO - a name chosen from a Greek word, isos that means equal, rather than an acronym). Since its formation in 1947 the ISO has published more than 16 500 international standards for all types of industry except electro-technology. The ISO works closely with international and governmental organizations, including national standards organizations in 157 countries all over the world.

In some countries standards are freely available, though in many countries they must be purchased from the regulatory body, ANSI or the SABS for example. Some have libraries that are open to the public where you can go and read the parts relevant to your project. However if you are employing the services of a professional designer of some sort (see box Role of the professional, opposite) this person ought to have copies of all the necessary codes and standards.

In addition to codes, regulations and standards, there is a universal need to ensure that structures - including carports and garages - do not encroach on other people's property, or on areas that are owned by the local authority, streets and sidewalks for example.

Also, you can generally be sure that certain building restrictions apply everywhere. For instance, building will not be allowed outside prescribed building lines without permission, and site plans must generally show these lines (including any servitudes) as well as all dimensions and boundaries. Building codes and regulations are normally quite specific concerning minimum requirements for drainage, fire protection, general structural arrangements (including foundations, details of damp-proofing and the location and levels of paved areas adjacent to the building), and contours of the property (including vehicle driveway levels and gradients). Both existing and proposed ground surfaces, as well as the surface of the public street at the boundary of the site, must usually be indicated on plans which are submitted for approval.

All cities, towns and communities have zoning ordinances or zoning schemes that govern things like how close you may build to a neighbor's boundary or property line; how far from the sidewalk you may build; how high any structure (including walls, fences and carports) may be; the maximum ground area that buildings and any structures on the property may cover (this is sometimes called the lot coverage or the land unit area permitted); and what procedures need to be followed should a property owner wish to apply for a variance (for example to build closer to a property line or boundary than normally permitted). There may also be specific parking requirements in a zoning ordinance, for instance a need for covered off-street parking, which may be why you are wanting to build a carport in the first place).

Another aspect to consider is that local authorities and building departments often have differing opinions as to what exactly constitutes a carport. Some authorities and building departments will allow the building of certain carport structures without plans - commonly because they define some projects as minor building work. So you might find that basic open-sided structures for cars, caravans and boats that are smaller than a specified size (let's say 40 m^2 or 430 ft^2) do not require plans, even if they are covered.

With all this in mind, it's best to check what is allowed before you even start planning. You should also be sure what paper-work will be required. Even if you don't need plans, you might need permits or some other type of written permission or authorization.

This is also a good place to mention the need to plan ahead (see box, Planning for the future, page 18). If for instance you think you might convert the carport to a garage at a later stage, plans invariably will be required. Also you will need foundations for walls, and footings if this is a pole structure. These must be constructed before laying your ground surface, as the foundation will not provide the necessary support if it is simply added on around the edges of the carport structure later. Rather incorporate foundations now than rip up the surface later.

Security & Lighting

These days, with an ever-increasing number of car thefts and assaults taking place much too close to home, security is an essential consideration when planning your carport. While gates may be added later, when budget allows, a little extra thought should be given to lighting in the planning stages. You might also want to consider anti-theft devices that prevent would-be thieves pushing or driving the car out of its parking place.

LIGHTING

If your house already has external lighting (which is a priority not just for security but for safety reasons as well), examine its effectiveness in terms of the carport you intend to build. Does it light up the site of the planned structure? Will it enable you to get from your car to the house without tripping over obstacles in the dark?

If there is no suitable external or garden lighting on your property already, consider a spotlight of some kind mounted on the wall of your house, and/or a light in the carport itself. When choosing lights, remember that they can have decorative qualities as well as practical advantages, and above all, that they should be energy efficient.

All electrical work should be undertaken, or at least closely supervised, by a qualified and registered electrician. However, there is generally nothing to stop you laying cables and fixing fittings yourself provided the wiring is connected to the grid by an authorized person. who knows what he is doing It is also imperative that all outdoor lighting is absolutely safe, since electricity and rain are a lethal combination. Only use weatherproof light fittings, even if the light is to be installed under the carport roof, and never use ordinary flex. If the structure is directly adjacent to the house, special PVC cable will be adequate. If the wiring extends across open ground, wired-steel armoured cable must be used, and should be buried at least 450 mm or 18 inches below the surface of the ground.

ABOVE
Today many homeowners are fitting CCTV cameras that point at their driveways and carports to monitor and record any activity.

TOP RIGHT
Strip lighting placed under the the roof of a carport will usually supply sufficient light for the interior.

RIGHT
The lamppost in front of this carport lights up both the carport and the surrounding area. It also gives character to the house and carport.

FAR RIGHT
Fold-down barriers provide protection against the theft of your car.

ABOVE LEFT
Gates make a reasonably efficient crime deterrent.

CENTER & LEFT
Remote controlled gates are even more effective since they prevent intruders from gaining access to the carport.

WAYS TO STAY SAFE & SECURE

Although it is not always a central issue when planning most outdoor structures, safety and security are of primary importance when a carport is sited on or near the boundary of any property - which is very common.

If the carport is to be situated within a walled or fenced area, away from the road, there may already be gates securing the area. But where there is direct access to the street, the most obvious solution is to install gates across the front of the carport. Remote-controlled gates are the best choice, as you don't have to climb in and out of the car every time you leave or return home, and so you will be less vulnerable; however they are also an expensive option. Another more elaborate possibility is to build in garage doors, or even automatic doors, on the boundary. This will, in a way, give you the best of both worlds - security without the expense and encumbrance of an actual building.

A very cheap and simple, but fairly effective, way of securing a carport without a gate is to fix a chain from pillar to pillar. Alternatively, a plain wooden boom can be fixed across the front. Metal fold-down barriers which are bolted to the surface are also available. Bear in mind that while these procedures will protect your vehicle from being stolen, they will still allow a thief access to the car and will therefore not safeguard radios, DVD players or other items that may have been left inside.

If your house already has external lighting examine its effectiveness in terms of security. If it is not adequate, you may consider installing security switches, which turn lights on and off automatically, and which are useful both inside and outside the house. There are various sorts available, all of which will suggest to potential burglars that there is someone at home at all times. Fixed time switches, controlled by a programmable unit, are particularly useful for patios, pathways and so on. Light- sensing devices, on the other hand, are a better option for carports and entrances. These are activated by natural light, and will automatically come on at dusk and turn off at dawn. Although the better units are connected to electrical circuit boards, cheaper external light fittings that are triggered in the same way are also available.

Many security systems also incorporate lighting that is activated automatically by movement, using passive infrared sensors. The lights and sensors can sometimes be bought from a DIY store for home fitting.

ABOVE
Automatic garage doors secure a carport from the road.

CHAPTER TWO
Costing Projects

Quantifying & Costing

Once you have settled on a design, and sorted out your plans, you will need to work out quantities of materials required, and then cost the project. If you choose to adapt one of the plans given on pages 55 to 61, you may need to alter the given quantities accordingly.

Use working drawings submitted to your local authority, or do your own sketches to scale. The more detailed the drawings are, the more accurately you can determine costs. List all the materials you will need, and increase quantities of bricks, cement and so on (including those listed for the plans) by about ten percent to allow for wastage and breakage.

BRICKS AND BLOCKS

Although brick sizes vary slightly, you can assume that 110 bricks will be enough for a square meter (11 ft²) of one-brick walling 222 mm (8¾ in) thick, and 55 bricks for half-brick or single walls.

To determine the number of bricks in a pillar, divide the height of the pillar by that of the brick plus mortar joint to assess how many courses you will need, then multiply by the number of bricks used in each course. A 2.4 m (7 ft 10 in) two-brick pillar, built with four 222 mm x 106 mm x 70 mm (8¾ in x 4 in x 2¾ in) bricks in each course and 10 mm (⅜ in) mortar joints, will use 120 bricks. If the structure has four pillars, you will need 480 bricks for the pillars.

The number of blocks needed to build a wall or pillar depends on the size of the blocks used. The blocks used for the carport on page 43 measure 390 mm x 190 mm x 190 mm (1 ft 3 in x 7 ½ in x 7 ½ in), and about 13 of these are required for each square meter (11 ft²) of wall.

If your blocks are a different size, multiply the length (plus mortar joint) by the height (plus mortar joint), and divide the result into 1,000,000 if working in mm, or divide the result in square inches into 1,296 - the number of square inches in a square yard. Alternatively, calculate the surface area of your proposed wall and divide by the size of one block. Apply the same principle used for bricks to work out how many blocks you will need for pillars.

Perforated decorative screen walling blocks are usually 290 mm x 290 mm x 90 mm or 100 mm (11⅜ in x 11⅜ in x 3½ in or 4 in) and you will need 11 blocks for every square meter (11 ft²). To lay a square meter (11 ft²) of brick paving you will need about 45 pavers.

CEMENT

You will need cement for concrete slabs and foundations, as well as mortar, and plaster or render if needed.

For major building projects one would order ready-mixed concrete according to the compressive strength required, but simple mix proportions are adequate for most home improvement brickwork projects. If you use 19 mm (¾ in) stone for foundations and footings, a cement:sand:stone mix in the ratio 1:4:4 (by volume) will yield about 5¼ units of measurement; adjust the ratio to 1:4:3 for smaller 13.2 mm (½ in) stone. If you are building fairly substantial walls, a slightly stronger 1:3:4 mix is recommended for the foundations. For every cubic meter or 35 ft³ of foundations you will need 4½-5 bags (225-250 kg or 505-560 lb). If you are casting a concrete floor, use a 1:2:3 mix - you will need about eight bags of cement per cubic meter (35 ft³).

ABOVE
A selection of bricks, blocks and pavers. Check what is available in your area that will suit your design and style.

RIGHT
Bricks, cement and some sand on site ready to start constructing pillars for a carport. The wheelbarrow and flat spade are essential tools to move sand, stone and bags of cement closer to where they are needed.

PREVIOUS PAGE
It is essential to get your initial calculations right if you are going to establish and stick to a budget.

If mixing by hand, it is preferable to work out quantities required per bag of cement (50 kg or 112 lb), for which you will need 150 litres (33 gal) each of sand and stone (for a 1:4:4 mix). The yield will be about 205 litres (45 gal).

When mixing mortar, you can count on using one bag for every 200 bricks in a half-brick wall, or 150 bricks in a one-brick wall (which has a double skin of brickwork). Mix cement with sand in the ratio 1:4 (by volume), or if lime is added, 2:1:8 for cement:lime:sand. If you are using 390 mm x 190 mm x 190 mm (1 ft 3 in x 7½ in x 7½ in) blocks, a weaker 1:6 cement:sand mixture is adequate and you will need about one bag for every 100 blocks. As you will use about 12½ blocks per square meter (11 ft²) of wall, 50 kg (112 lb) of cement should be enough to build about 8 m² (86 ft²).

The same mix ratios may be used for plaster, which will then match the strength of the mortar. It should be 10-15 mm (about ½ in) thick, and you will need about 4 kg (9 lb) of cement for every square meter (11 ft²).

Pillars are seldom left hollow, so you will need extra cement for concrete to fill in the central cavity - unless you are building solid, one-brick square piers.

SAND

Quantifying sand by volume is never very accurate because sands differ and their moisture content varies. The mass of sand per cubic meter (35 ft³) is roughly 1,350 kg (2,976 lb).

Using a 1:4 cement:sand mix for both mortar and plaster, for every 100 bricks of one-brick wall you lay you will need 100 litres (22 gal) or about 2½ 50 kg (112 lb) bags of sand. For plastering, 12 litres (2 ⅔ gal) or 16 kg (35 lb) will be enough for each square meter (11 ft²).

If there is a lot of brickwork and you order in bulk, a cubic meter of sand (35 ft³) is enough for laying 1,000 bricks or plastering 84 m² (900 ft²) of wall. Sand is also required for concrete slabs and foundations. Work out quantities according to the ratios specified.

Sand must be clean and can be ordered by volume and delivered by the truck load or bought in bags for smaller jobs. For a slab, a 1:2:3 cement:sand:stone ratio is recommended. Alter this to 1:2:2 if you are working with the smaller stone.

Paving bricks and blocks should be laid on a layer of building sand 25-50 mm (1-2 in) thick. At a thickness of 40 mm (1½ in), as specified in the plans on pages 55 to 61, one cubic meter (35 ft³) will cover 25 m² (269 ft²). You will need slightly more to brush over the surface once paving is complete (see pages 51 to 54). Some people advocate brushing on a 1:6 cement: sand mix instead of pure sand.

STONE

As the vital coarse aggregate used for making concrete, crushed stone or gravel is essential for all foundations and solid slabs. The quantity will depend partly on the size of stone you use - relevant proportions were detailed previously. For the designs in this book, the requirements presume you are using 19 mm (¾in) stone.

BINDERS

If you use plaster sand with a lime content for mortar and plaster, no extra lime is needed. Note that adding lime to ordinary builder's sand to improve its binding quality will give a slightly higher yield if you use the same cement:sand mix proportions. Alternatively, add 50 ml (2 fl oz) of plasticiser to every 50 kg (112 lb) of cement. For small projects, use a tablespoon of good quality liquid soap as a substitute.

TIMBER

It is almost always cheaper to buy timber in standard lengths. Check what is available before designing your structure - or adapt the require-ler lengths are to be used (for a screen or railings, for instance), buy whatever lengths will give you the least wastage. If the lengths used in the plans on pages 55 to 61 are not available, buy longer pieces and cut to size.

ROOFING MATERIALS

Many roofing materials are available in only a few standard widths. Instead of cutting the sheets (which may be difficult to handle), it is usually possible to design a structure utilising the full expanse. This simplifies construction and cuts down on time and labour.

GUTTERS AND DOWNPIPES

To ensure effective drainage, guttering is installed on structures with a solid roof covering, often on one side only, to catch the run-off from a sloping roof. Some designs include concealed gutters, adjacent to the fascia board or at the back of the structure between wall and beam. A downpipe, the length of a pillar or post, takes water from the gutter to a channel or drain. Remember to buy the correct brackets and connectors to fit these components.

OTHER COSTS

If you are planning to enlist the help of professional builders or artisans, include their fee in your final costing. Rather overestimate their time, otherwise you may throw out the budget at a crucial time and jeopardise the entire project.

Budget for materials such as tiles, reinforcing and connectors, finishing touches like paint and plants, and any tools you need to buy. Also add in a figure for removing excess soil and rubble.

ABOVE
Suppliers will deliver truck loads of stone and sand to site. It usually works out cheaper buying this way, providing the quantities you need warrants it.

PLANNING FOR THE FUTURE

It is always a good idea to plan for the future, or at least think ahead in terms of what may be done to a carport structure at a later stage to improve or change it. Even if it is not something you think you are likely to do, always consider the implications for resale. People buying property often think of potential when they evaluate whether or not to submit an offer to purchase. So for instance while there may not be a garage, if there is a carport that can easily be converted into a garage, this could sway the sale.

Bear in mind that a conversion will potentially be cheaper than scrapping an existing structure and rebuilding from scratch.

So if a carport has a good, solid roof with gutters and a downpipe to enable rainwater to drain away, you already have the makings of a garage. Remember though that if the conversion involves a bricks and mortar addition, you will need foundations. And if the carport floor has to be dug up to accommodate this, it may be false economy.

Since plans will usually be required to build a garage, it may be a good idea to formulate these when you build the carport, even if you don't submit them.

Ultimately consider the space available and think out of the box in terms of what can be done with it now and later.

ABOVE & LEFT
What was originally a carport has been cleverly converted to a double garage. The sides are made of corrugated sheeting, so there was no need for extra foundations. to support walls

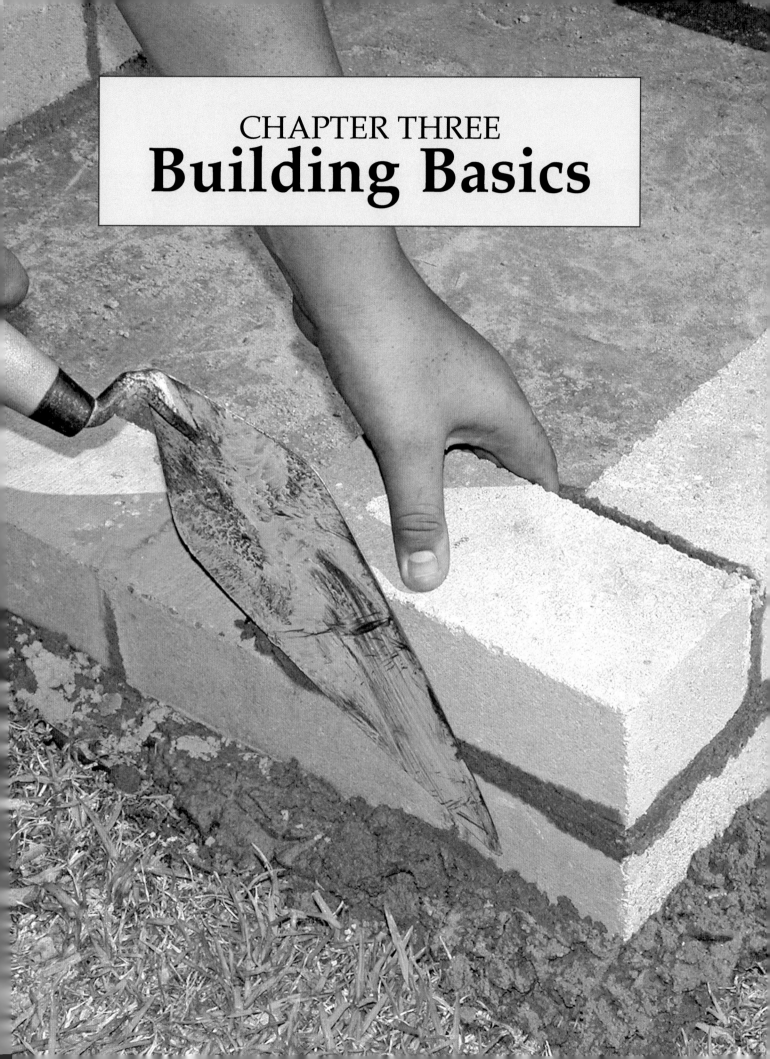

CHAPTER THREE
Building Basics

Construction Principles

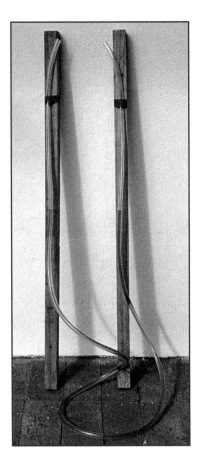

ABOVE
A simple homemde water level
is an invaluable tool when
tackling any building project.

RIGHT
A level is an indispensable tool
when doing any brickwork or
blockwork to check not only
that each brick or block is level
but also if the wall or pillar is
vertical and plumb. It is also
essential for concretework.

PREVIOUS PAGE
Basic bricklaying skills are useful
for some of the projects
featured in this book.

The design and style you choose for any garden structure will determine the materials required, but before you start, you must ensure that you can master the relevant techniques and confidently handle all the tools needed to work with the materials. you have chosen

The basic construction principles and methods used to erect a simple carport are certainly within the capabilities of most handy men and women. The secret is to familiarize yourself with the rudiments involved, and stick to them while you work.

THE BASICS

Common sense will tell you that all components need to be vertical and level.

Supporting poles must not tilt; bricks and blocks must be laid level and square (at 90 degrees); and paving must be flat, level and even on the surface. You may be working with the best quality materials, but if you do not ensure that your workmanship is square, level and plumb, you will not achieve the professional kind of finish that we all appreciate.

Square If the corners of a structure are at right angles, it will be square. While almost always applicable when building with bricks or blocks, this principle will not be relevant if the carport design is not rectangular or square for some strange reason.

When setting out a design with right-angled corners, it is simple to check that it is square by using the 3:4:5 method (see page 23). When you build up the brickwork you will need to use a builder's square, which will enable you to check constantly that the rising corners are at 90 degrees.

Level In brickwork, all horizontal surfaces must be absolutely level. You can ensure this by checking foundations and footings, as well as each brick course you lay, with a spirit level. If the bubble in the horizontal vial is centred, the surface is level. When using this useful tool on large surfaces (when paving or throwing a concrete slab, for instance) it is common practice to set the spirit level on a long straight-edged piece of wood.

A line level may be used to ensure that brick pillars are progressing evenly, or to check that a builder's line is correctly positioned.

Paved areas should slope slightly for drainage, and you will have to take this into account. When paving, it is therefore helpful to set up a line corresponding with the slope of the finished surface. Do not rely on guesswork; instead, use a spacer block under your spirit level or straightedge to keep the angle consistent, and then set up the line. To achieve a gradient of 1 in 40, use a 25 mm (1 in) block of wood for each meter (3 ft 3 in).

You can also use a water level to set up a drainage slope, or for that matter to ensure that your building site is level. This method is particularly useful over a long stretch or when you need to ensure consistency around a corner. All you need is transparent tubing that is long enough for the requirements of your project, or an ordinary hosepipe with small pieces of transparent tubing fitted in each end. Fill the tube or hosepipe with water and attach it to two pegs set in the ground at any given height. Since water finds its own level, you will immediately see whether to remove more earth or to fill in.

A water level is also invaluable when building a structure with timber uprights. Once you have concreted the posts into the ground, use it to check that the tops are exactly level with one another. If not, simply saw off enough wood to make them the same height.

Plumb Vertical surfaces of all walls and timber posts must also be aligned and level. A spirit level with both a vertical and a horizontal vial is most commonly used to check for plumb. Alternatively, you can use a plumb bob, which is especially useful for ensuring that the corners of brick or block pillars are straight and upright.

FOUNDATIONS

If you are building with bricks and mortar, timber or metal, all upright pillars and poles must be securely anchored or constructed on a sound footing.

You will also need to dig and place strip foundations for any walls or screens included in your carport design, and you may have to construct a concrete slab prior to paving if the ground is unstable.

Minimum dimensions for foundations and footings are specified by various building standards (see box Building codes & regulations, page 11).

Concrete A basic concrete mix consists of cement, sand, stone and water, often combined with plasticiser to make it more pliable. Use ordinary Portland cement, widely available in sealed 50 kg (112 lb) bags; together with clean building sand (called sharp sand in some countries) sold in bags of about 50 kg (112 lb), or supplied in bulk by the cubic meter or cubic foot; 19 mm (¾ in) or 13.2 mm (½ in) crushed stone or gravel; and potable tap water.

Dry premixed materials are also available. These are very useful for small projects, including footings for some carports. Purchasing concrete this way, however, is more expensive than buying the constituent materials individually.

The quantities and proportions you use will depend on the work to be done. However, low-strength concrete is quite adequate for the foundation of most simple structures. If you are working with 19 mm (¾ in) stone, the recommended proportions of cement, sand and stone for hand compaction are 1:4:4, measured by volume. If you opt for a smaller 13.2 mm (½ in) stone, which is certainly easier to mix by hand, less stone should be used - alter the proportions to 1:4:3. If a stronger mix is required, a suitable ratio for the larger stone is 1:3:3, and for the smaller stone, 1:3:2. If necessary you can consult an engineer who will advise.

There is no need to measure the water to be used. Simply mix the cement and sand together until the color is uniform; form a hollow in the middle and add a small amount of liquid at a time, shovelling from the outsides to the centre until you have a workable consistency. Add the stone last, with a little more water if the concrete is too dry.

When using a concrete mixer, load the stone first, together with some water. This prevents cement from building up around the blades of the machine. Add the cement next, and then the sand and enough water to achieve a soft, porridgey consistency.

If you are sinking metal or timber posts into the ground, these must be supported with some form of bracing to ensure that they are absolutely vertical and do not fall over. Once you have checked for plumb with a spirit level, shovel the concrete into the hole and tamp down well with the back of your shovel to compact it and expel all air bubbles.

Foundations for brickwork must be allowed to set before building commences. The concrete must be kept moist while it is curing - hose it lightly with water or cover it with hessian or plastic. Avoid exposure to drying winds, hot sunshine and frost. Ideally, it should be left to cure for five to seven days, although in practice building often begins a day or two after throwing the foundations.

ABOVE LEFT
A small quantity of concrete is mixed in a builder's wheelbarrow. Note that an ordinary gardener's wheelbarrow is too small and shallow for mixing concrete.

ABOVE RIGHT
Mortar is placed on the surface of newly cured but well set concrete.

Dimensions The dimensions of foundations and footings will depend on your particular design, as well as soil conditions in your garden. Nevertheless, they should always be at least 200 mm (8 in) deep, and more substantial if a heavy roof is to be incorporated for protection.

A useful rule of thumb when estimating the width of any foundation for brickwork or blockwork is that it should equal the thickness of the wall or pillar plus twice the depth of the concrete. So a 200 mm (8 in) deep footing for a 400 mm x 400 mm (1 ft 4 in x 1 ft 4 in) pillar should be at least 800 mm (2 ft 8 in) wide. If you are in any doubt, increase the size of the footing or get professional advice.

While some people bed wooden poles directly into the ground, compacting around the poles to stabilise them, it is best to set poles in concrete. In fact, a concrete foundation is essential if the structure has a solid roof, as uplift (which occurs when wind gusts under the roof) could result in damage if it is not securely anchored.

Metal poles should always be bedded in reasonably substantial footings at least 600 mm (2 ft) deep, while the base of precast concrete pillars should also be set in a concrete foundation.

When digging foundations for poles, it may be tempting to use a mechanical auger. However, this tool will excavate a hole that is smaller than the size recommended for foundations, which in turn will affect the strength of the foundations. If you do use one, you will have to bore much deeper into the ground to prevent the pole from coming loose.

Above-ground Anchorage When working with wood, the most common alternative to setting the base in a concrete footing is to use metal base plates. Many people prefer above-ground anchorage as it reduces the likelihood of wood rot. Various anchor plates for posts are available off-the-shelf for cut timber, but you will probably have to get an engineering firm to make something to secure wooden poles, for instance sturdy galvanized iron bent in an L-shape.

Whatever form of anchorage you use, unless you already have a solid base, you will need to throw a foundation slab or footing onto which it can be fixed. While a concrete slab might be thinner, the minimum depth for footings is usually 200 mm (8 in). Alternatively you can use a tube form that will give you a neat finish, even if the concrete shows above ground. These are made of cardboard and are available in several sizes. If the footing extends above ground level, any visible tubing should be removed once the concrete has set.

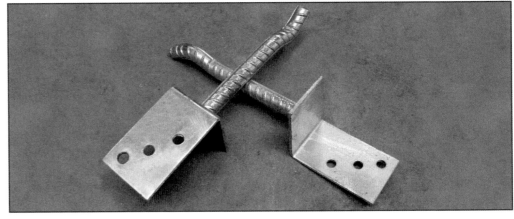

ABOVE LEFT
Posts for a timber-framed carport are anchored on the concrete slab, slightly above ground.

ABOVE RIGHT
A concrete pad footing has metal anchors set into the concrete ready for the upright posts to be securely attached.

RIGHT
Specially designed post anchors.

SETTING OUT

The first step in any building project is to set out the site according to the dimensions and layout of your plan, this essential so that you know your siting is correct.

The first step is to ensure that each corner you set out is exactly square. The simplest way of doing this is to use the 3:4:5 method, as shown in the photograph below.

Setting out a carport measuring 4 m x 3.5 m (13 ft x 11 ft 6 in) from outer corner to outer corner of the pillars, is a relatively easy procedure The dimensions of the footings will depend on the structure itself; in this case the pillars, to be built from concrete blocks, will measure 400 mm x 400 mm (1 ft 4 in x 1 ft 4 in). To support these, foundation footings should measure 800 mm x 800 mm (2 ft 8 in x 2 ft 8 in) across, and about 300 mm (1 ft) deep. If you draw the dimensions to a smaller scale on paper first, you will see that the distances between the inner sides of the pillars will be 3.2 m (10 ft 6 in) and 2.7 m (8 ft 10 in). 200 mm (8 in) of each footing will therefore extend beyond the framework at each corner.

Having decided on the location of the carport, knock a peg into the ground at one corner. Then, using a steel square or a wooden square (see Tools, page 33), measure 3.5 m (11 ft 6 in) in one direction and 4 m (13 ft) at right angles to this line. Insert a peg in the ground at each of these points.

To check the angle using the 3:4:5 method, knock another peg into the ground 3 m (10 ft) from the corner on the shorter side, and then measure the distance between this peg and the one already inserted 4 m (13 ft) from the corner. This peg should be exactly 5 m (16 ft 4 in) away from the 3 m peg. If not, adjust the angle slightly until the measurement, and therefore the angle, is correct. This can be substituted with imperial measurements, 3 ft x 4 ft x 5 ft.

Now measure the other two sides and knock a peg into the ground where they meet. Check all the corners to ensure that each one is at 90 degrees. To double-check that the corners are in fact square, measure the diagonals. These should be the same length and, in this case, should measure just over 5.3 m (17 ft 4 in).

To work out the distance mathematically, determine the square root of (side A^2 + side B^2), that is, $\sqrt{(3.5 \text{ m})^2 + (4 \text{ m})^2}$ = 5.315 m ($\sqrt{(11 \text{ ft } 6 \text{ in})^2 + (13 \text{ ft})^2}$ = 17.357 ft, or 17 ft 4¼ in).

The next step is to mark the position of the holes for all four footings. For accuracy you should mark them before they are dug out. You can use lime, white cement, chalk or even flour to do this.

The easiest method is to take your pegs and set up a builder's line along the perimeter of the building site, extending beyond the corners by 200 mm (8 in). Pull the string taut, then using the line as a guide, mark the ground 600 mm (2 ft) from each peg, in both directions. Finally, using a builder's square for accuracy, draw four squares using the points you have marked.

ABOVE
To set out the structure built step-by-step on pages 43 to 46, pegs were knocked into the ground at each corner and the foundation footings marked with flour. The yellow line indicates the outside edge of the structure since the foundations are 200 mm (8 in) wider than the pillars on all sides. A red peg was inserted to check for square as described above.

BRICKS AND MORTAR

While it is quite possible to erect carports without using brickwork anywhere, brick and block walls, piers and pillars are features that are often found in even the simplest designs.

The basic techniques required for bricklaying are reasonably easy to master, although, as with any other building techniques, it will take practice to perfect them.

Bricks and Blocks There is a wide range of bricks and blocks available that is suitable for carport structures. These include facebricks, clay and concrete bricks designed to be plastered, inexpensive concrete blocks that are also plastered or rendered, and reconstituted (or reconstructed) stone blocks that are made in imitation of natural stone. Although special tools and skills are required for cutting natural stone, this material may also be used.

Various bricks and blocks that are suitable for paving are discussed on page 42.

Mortar Both bricks and blocks are bonded together with mortar to give the structure maximum strength. While a range of suitable bonding patterns may be used for garden walls, pillars and piers are most commonly built using a stretcher bond. To achieve this bond, bricks are laid lengthways and those in each successive course overlap the bricks below by half. For the mortar you will need cement, sand (sometimes referred to as soft sand) and water. Use the same Portland cement recommended for concrete. This may be mixed with ordinary building sand (to which hydrated builder's lime should be added to improve the binding and water-retentive quality of the mixture) or plaster sand (which may already contain lime). In some areas, plasticiser is used instead of lime, and some people even use liquid soap as a substitute for smaller projects.

Dry premixed mortar is available too, although, like premixed concrete, it is generally considerably more expensive than buying the individual materials and mixing them yourself.

A suitable mix for general external brickwork is based on a cement:sand ratio of 1:4. Combine the dry materials and add water (as though you were making concrete, but without adding stone). The mixture is ready for use when it is of a uniform color and consistency, and when you can push a brick into it end-on with your hand. It should have a plastic texture and it should be sufficiently cohesive to achieve a good bond with the bricks.

Mix only enough mortar for immediate use. After about two hours it will start to stiffen and must be discarded. Never try to soften it later by adding more water as this will weaken the mixture and the structure could crumble.

Bricklaying The most important tool you need is a trowel, essential for lifting the mortar and buttering the bricks. In addition, you will need a spirit level and a builder's square, and you should also make a gauge rod (see page 34), which is invaluable for maintaining equal courses. For cutting bricks, use the chisel end of a brick hammer, or a bolster and hefty club hammer. If you are building with facebricks, you will also need a jointing tool to finish off the brickwork.

Before attempting to lay bricks for the first time, practice using the trowel. The technique is reasonably easy to master; the secret is to ensure that the brickwork remains square, level and plumb. For this reason it is essential to make frequent use of your spirit level, square and gauge rod (see pages 20 and 33).

Each brick course is bedded in mortar, which will bond better if slightly furrowed down the center. Butter the header or short end of the brick before sliding it into position; if there are any gaps, use a trowel to fill with more mortar. Tap the brick gently into place with the trowel handle until it is level, and then scrape off any excess mortar.

ABOVE RIGHT
A simple carport with white plastered pillars, built beside a garage.

Plaster or Render Unless pillars and piers have been built with facebricks, the surface should be plastered or rendered. Not only is a plaster finish decorative, but it will also make the structure more weatherproof.

Plaster or render is made in exactly the same way as mortar, but it is more important to add lime to the mixture. This helps to prevent cracking and gives the plaster or render a plastic quality, making it easier to apply. Plaster sand, which has a lime content, is therefore generally preferred. Newly built brickwork is usually perfect for plastering; if it is dusty or grimy, clean it thoroughly before work begins. It is also advisable to moisten the surface 24 hours before it is plastered or rendered to prevent too much water from being absorbed from the plaster mix.

Apply the plaster to the surface with a plasterer's trowel, pressing it down to ensure that it sticks. Leave it for about half an hour before scraping it to a uniform finish with a screed board; then smooth it with a wooden or steel float.

Use a corner trowel to neaten the corners. Take care not to over-trowel the surface as it can bring the finer material to the surface and cause cracking. While plaster is usually 10 to 15 mm (about a half inch) thick, uneven areas may require a thicker covering. If this is necessary, apply it in two coats. Let the first set, then scratch it to provide a key for the second.

Once plaster has been applied should not dry out too quickly, so keep it damp for two or three days by spraying it very lightly with a hose. Once the surface has dried, you can paint it; experts recommended that you use a primer and/or sealant first but it depends on the paint you use and on local climatic conditions.

ABOVE LEFT
Garage and carport walls have been plastered and painted to match the house.

CENTER LEFT
Plaster or render (basically a mortar mix) is applied to the surface of the blocks with a trowel.

CENTER RIGHT
Here the external (outer) corners of a plastered surface is smoothed off and finished with a special corner plaster tool. An internal corner tool has the opposite shape that enables smoothing into tight inside corners.

MIXING MORTAR

Mixing mortar is a very similar process to mixing concrete (see Chapter Five, Step-by-Step Concretework, pages 47 to 50). The main difference is that you don't add crushed stone or gravel to the dry materials. If mixing mortar by hand, work on a hard, clean surface that will not absorb the water. Never mix directly on soil or grass as the groundwill absorb moisture from the mixture and contaminate it. You can mix on asphalt, brick-paving or concrete surfaces, but hose the area down as soon as you have finished work to prevent the cement mixture from drying and staining the surface. A builder's wheelbarrow is suitable for smaller projects., otherwise use a concrete mixer.

When mixing by hand, spread the sand out first and then spread the cement on top. Working from the outside, shovel the mix into a pile in the center. Spread the mix outwards, and then shovel back to a pile in the center. Continue doing this until the sand and cement forms a consistent color. Next draw the mix to the outside of the pile and form what looks like a crater.; add clean water into the crater. Then start by shovelling small quantities of the mix back into the center and mix it with the water. Do this a few times until the mix is workable. Stop any water running away by damming up the wall with some of the mix. There is no need to measure the quantity of water used; start by adding small amounts of water at a time and just add enough to make the mix plastic and workable.

Too little water will make it difficult to work with and too much will make it obviously watery and will weaken the mix.

When using a concrete mixer for larger volumes of mortar, load some sand first with a little bit of water and run the machine for a few minutes. This prevents the mix from building up on the blades. Add the rest of the sand next, and then finally the cement. If the machine has a loading skip, you can add the cement before the sand. Once the dry materials have been loaded, it should only take a couple of minutes to thoroughly mix them together. Add a little more water. Make certain the concrete mixer is completely discharged and empty before you reload it as any left over mortar in the mix will affect the curing and drying time of the new batch..

TOP LEFT Measure the sand and cement out onto on a clean, dry surface. TOP RIGHT Mix the sand and cement until they form a uniform color. BELOW LEFT Make a small crater in the centre of the dry materials and add clean water gradually, shovelling the mixture into the crater. BELOW RIGHT Shovel the mixture from the edges to the centre to mix thoroughly. Continue to mix until all the materials are blended together. When the mix is soft and porridge-like it is ready for use.

BUILDING BRICK PIERS

For a four-brick or six-brick course pier:
1. Dig a hole at least 200 mm (8 in) deep and 600 mm x 600 mm (24 in x 24 in) wide (the dimensions of the hole are variable depending on the size of your pier).
2. Thoroughly mix your concrete using a ratio of 1:4:4 - cement:sand:stone (see page 49) and water.
3. Pour the concrete into the hole.
4. Put a mild-steel reinforcing rod (Y12) in the centre, making sure that the top of the rod is level with the proposed height of your pier, and prop it up with pieces of timber.
5. Leave overnight to allow the concrete to set.
6. Lay out your first course of bricks on the hardened concrete, to mark out the sides of your column.
7. Stretch string between pegs to demarcate two opposite sides of your column accurately.
8. Mark out the other two sides with a square, in order to get a 90 degree angle.
9. Remove the bricks and lay a bed of mortar (cement:sand ratio of 1:4 - see page 21) along the lines that you marked out where the pier is to be built.
10. Draw a trowel down the centre of the mortar to create a small furrow; this will give the bricks better purchase.
11. Lay out the first course of bricks according to top or third picture right, making sure that the gaps between them are equal.
12. Fill the gaps with mortar, and using a spirit level, check that the course is level.
13. Use a straight edged length of timber marked off at intervals equal to one brick plus mortar (about 85 mm - 3½ in) to check the height of each brick course.
14. Repeat the process from step 11 as shown in every second picture, right.
15. Continue the process until you reach the desired height, alternating the way the bricks are laid to bond them. Fill the centre of the pier with mortar as you work. diagrams), Constantly use the spirit level to check that the edges of the pier are level on top and vertical on the sides.
16. Allow seven days for the mortar to set and cure.

Pier with four bricks per course.

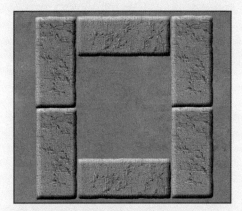

Pier with six bricks per course.

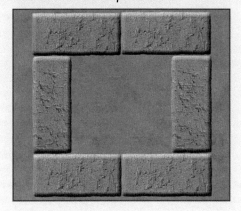

TIMBER

The type of wood or lumber chosen for any carport project will depend on what is available locally, what is required for your design, and on cost. With forest depletion in many parts of the world, the price of many woods has soared in recent years and some formerly common woods are now difficult to find.

Generally timber can be bought as poles or as cut wood (including laminated timber), both of which are suitable for a wide range of projects such as carports and other garden structures.

Cut Timber Both hardwoods (from deciduous trees) and softwoods (from conifers) may be used in the garden, although most woods must be treated in some way. Hardwood like teak is tough and will withstand most weather conditions, but few people can afford it; other less expensive hardwoods may be substituted. Suitable softwoods include redwood and cedar which are both naturally rot resistant, but also expensive. If pine is used is essential it is treated for structural use.

Various preservatives are used, most of which are applied under extreme pressure, although different countries favour certain specific products. These include pentachlorophenol and tributyl tin oxide - both organic substances. Generally speaking, if a wood has been treated according to recognised specifications, it will be suitable for construction purposes.

If you are treating your own timber, do so before construction, and ensure that it is thoroughly dry, otherwise the chemicals will not penetrate thoroughly (see opposite page).

Although rough-cut wood may be used for carports, it is generally better aesthetically to opt for planed timber or laminated beams. While the latter are more expensive, they are also stronger and more stable. Another advantage of using laminated timber is that it is available in much longer lengths, more than double the span of ordinary planks and beams. Cover strips (thin, flat strips of wood) or half-round strips of timber may also be useful for securing shadecloth and awning material in position and preventing it from lifting in heavy wind.

Never accept wood that is badly warped or cracked. While small knots are unavoidable in many woods, it is best to avoid boards with very large knots, as the knot will often fall out, and this can adversely affect the strength of your structure.

While the roof structure of most buildings consists of a number of components (beams, trusses, rafters, battens and so on), the configuration of carport roofs is usually simple. Such a structure typically has beams supporting crosspieces or purlins, which in turn hold up the roof sheeting, if this is used. Some structures may also have battens, which are usually smaller than purlins.

Poles There is a charming rusticity about carports built with poles. Using poles does not limit the usefulness of the structure, and they may be combined with cut timber, for example, to create a more sophisticated and elaborate shelter with a solid roof structure.

Usually there is a choice between poles that have simply been debarked, and those which have been machined to a smooth surface, making them reasonably regular in size. Split poles, which are useful if you wish to incorporate railings or screen a section of the carport, are also available commercially. Whatever you choose, it is best to opt for poles that have been treated against infestation and rot.

Traditionally, hardwood poles were dipped in or coated with creosote, a dark brown oil distilled from coal tar and considered for many years to be the best wood-preservative. If it is not pressure-treated, though, it wears off and must be regularly reapplied. It is also toxic to plants and will cause some materials, including shadecloth, to rot.

Today, many sawmills impregnate poles with substances which enable the wood to resist pests and withstand damp conditions. One of the most common of these substances is chromated copper arsenate (CCA), a water-based preservative that usually gives wood a slight green tinge. It is though being phased out in many countries because of its arsenic content.

Poles that have not been treated should at least be coated at one end with a bituminous waterproofing compound, or some other environmentally friendly preservative that will prevent them from deteriorating too rapidly when buried in the ground.

Working with Wood One of the attractions of a wooden structure is that it is reasonably simple for the amateur DIY enthusiast to erect. If you have an aptitude for making things and can use a drill and a saw, you are already halfway there.

You do not need an elaborate toolkit, and can even make a simple structure with hand tools alone. The minimum equipment you will need is a saw, steel tape measure, drill (an inexpensive hand drill will suffice), screwdriver, hammer, and of course the tools required to ensure that the poles, posts and beams are square, level and plumb (see page 20). Power tools will, of course, simplify the task. If you do not have any tools, consider how much you will use them in future, as well as how much you can afford to spend, before going shopping. Also investigate the possibility of hiring tools.

Finishes Most timber, especially softwood that has been cut and planed, needs additional protection if it is to look attractive and last for a reasonable length of time. While a good quality hardwood will weather to a gentle gray color without losing its strength and stability, softwoods like pine should always be varnished or painted. If you are planning to paint or seal your pergola or carport, ensure that the preservative you use is compatible with the finishing coat - some treatments cannot be overcoated.

Perhaps the simplest coating is a penetrating oil preservative dressing that will waterproof the wood and protect it against the weather, rot and insect attack. These dressings are easy to apply but, because they are not resistant to sunlight, have to be reapplied every six to nine months. They are also more suitable for use on hardwoods than on softwoods. Although it is not a preservative dressing as such, linseed oil will 'feed' the wood, and can be used on its own on some hardwoods.

Exterior sealers and varnish, which comes in various shades and both matt and gloss finishes, is generally UV-resistant as well as waterproof. A good quality product will last for several years before it needs to be reapplied.

Alternatively, you can paint the wood. There are numerous types of paint from which to choose, although the most usual kind found on outdoor structures is ordinary gloss paint, that will give you a tough, durable surface in a vast range of colors. In addition to two coats of gloss paint you will first have to use a good quality primer and coat the wood first to protect it and aid adhesion, and then give it a suitable undercoat before your top coat.

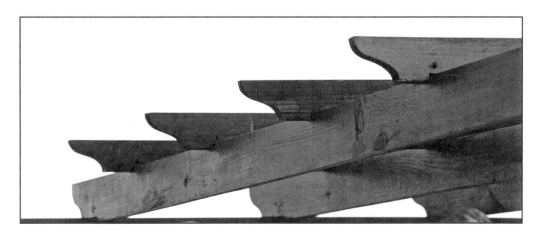

LEFT
Timber beams have been coated with an exterior sealer for protection.

OTHER MATERIALS

While brick and timber (or lumber) are certainly the most common materials used for the upright framework of carports and pergolas, these are by no means the only options.

Precast concrete A practical and attractive choice, precast concrete pillars are well suited to carports and other garden structures. They are available in a variety of styles and heights, and if you wish, they may be concreted on to a precast plinth or a brick base to raise their height. These pillars usually have built-in reinforcing on to which the roof beams or horizontal poles are bolted.

Metal Galvanized steel poles are commonly used for carports, and less frequently, for pergolas. Poles should be at least 38 mm (1½in) in diameter, and they should be set in reasonably substantial footings or bolted into a base plate and post connector which has been attached to or anchored into a concrete slab (see pages 21 and 22).

Rectangular or square aluminum tubing is sometimes used for carport construction. However, it is not a common material for do-it-yourself projects.

Fiber-cement Piping made from fiber-cement is a more unusual, but quite acceptable, material. It may be used in the same way as poles, with fatter pipes forming the uprights, and thinner ones the crossbeams. (see page 7) The uprights should be reinforced and filled with concrete.

ABOVE RIGHT
A simple timber carport erected in front of a double garage provides dappled shade for vehicles that park under it.

RIGHT
Precast concrete pillars have been used to support straightforward wooden beams.

FAR RIGHT
An all-metal carport erected in front of a double garage for additional protection.

Support Specifications

The upright framework of the carport - the poles and pillars which support the roof - is often made of brick or timber, though galvanized metal, aluminum or precast-concrete pillars may also be used (see Other Materials, opposite). There are also many different ways that the uprights may be attached to whatever roof structure is chosen.

SPECIFICATIONS FOR UPRIGHTS

The size and nature of the structure will determine the dimensions of the materials used. If a solid roof is to be erected, it is essential that the upright supports are able to take the weight of the roof. It must also be able to withstand the 'stretching' action that takes place when wind gusts under the roof.

ANCHORAGE

Building codes and regulations specify minimum dimensions for concrete footings and foundations relating to both wood and brick structures, though local authorities do sometimes enforce more stringent specifications. This is to ensure that the structure will be stable and safe, and will not be effected by wind loads or other factors that could cause it to collapse.

Generally low-strength concrete (a 1:4:4 mix of cement:sand:stone) may be used for most structures (see pages 16 and 17 for other mix ratios). A layer of stone should be placed at the bottom of each footing to allow water to drain.

If the carport structure incorporates brick or block pillars or shorter piers, a 225 mm deep (8¾ in) foundation about 600 mm (23½ in) wide should be adequate for most structures. These dimensions should be specified on your carport plans. A basic knowledge of bricklaying is necessary to build the piers (see box Building brick piers, page 27).

If precast-concrete pillars are chosen they may be placed on a precast-concrete or brick base to raise the height if necessary. Alternatively the base of the pillar will be sunk into the ground.

Metal poles should be set in substantial footings at least 600 mm (23½ in) deep or bolted into a baseplate and post connector attached to an existing slab (see Post-slab connections, page 32). The poles should have a diameter of about 38 mm (1½ in) or more.

FIXING AND FASTENING

There are numerous fastening aids available in the building trade, including truss and joist hangers, galvanized T-hinges, wall plates, bolts, clamps, couplings, screws and rivets. Where possible, stainless steel, aluminum or galvanized materials should be used to minimize the possibility of these elements rusting or staining the structure.

You will find that a variety of cuphead bolts and washers, coach screws, wire nails and other hardware will be needed for projects. Crosspieces and uprights are usually bolted or screwed together, although nails can sometimes be used. Beams can be held together with clips, grips and joist hangers. Truss hangers can be used to fix beams to a wall. Uprights can be fastened to specially manufactured ppost anchor bases that are attached to concrete with expanding bolts or anchor bolts. Angle iron can be customized to

ABOVE
Ordinary truss hangers are ideal for carports that are constructed alongside a building.

LEFT
A metal pole has been welded to a support bracket that is used to hold the beams in place.

ABOVE LEFT
Upright poles are bolted to the
main beams of this carport;
purlins are slotted into notches
and nailed down. (See plan 1 on
page 56)

ABOVE RIGHT
A post anchor bolted in place
is used to fix the support to the
ground.

CENTER
Instead of digging a hole for
your carport uprights you can
build short brick piers and
anchor wooden or metal posts
in the center.

RIGHT
Pre-drilled metal has been
concreted into the top of a
precast pillar to secure the
overhead beams.

FAR RIGHT
Galvanized hoop iron is a cheap
and easy method of attaching
beams to supports.

attach timber to walls, and both clamps and galvanized hoop iron are useful for securing roof structures.

It is essential that bolts and screws are long enough to go right through any timber that has to be secured and supported. If they are too long use a hacksaw to cut them once they in place.

Framework Connections
• Beam bolt plates may be used to attach posts to roof beams.
• Metal angle-strips may be used to attach wooden beams and posts to one another.
• Wall plates and truss hangers may be fitted to walls to act as supports for your carport roof.
• Expanded masonry anchor bolts may be put into walls for roof supports.
• Wood joints are surprisingly simple and a good way of fixing crossbeams and rafters. Simply notch out the beam to fit the rafter.
• Semicircular clamps or hoop iron brackets are

particularly useful for securing gum poles.
• V-shaped gavanized connectors, which bolt together, may also be used for gum poles.

Post-slab Connections
• A baseplate may be used with some post connectors: bolt the plate to an existing concrete slab.
• Expanding bolts (40 mm-100 mm or 1½ in-4 in concrete wedge anchors) can be used to attach baseplates to a slab.
• Anchor bolts may be put into position when the concrete is still wet, or bolted in later.
• Short brick piers eliminate the need to bed timber into foundation concrete.

If you are using metal or timber poles or posts, and already have a concrete floor to your carport, it is often advisable to chisel the concrete out with a cold chisel and club hammer, and sink the uprights into the hole before securing them with fresh concrete.

Tools

Do-it-yourself enthusiasts usually have a selection of tools which will be quite adequate for all of the projects described. in this book Most are available from DIY or hardware stores, although a few will have to be made at home. If you do not want to buy new tools, they can often be hired at a reasonable daily rate.

SETTING OUT & LEVELLING

Essential equipment needed for setting out your site, and for ensuring that your structure is square, level and plumb, must be included in your basic toolkit for any building job. In addition, you will need to use a good quality retractable tape measure at all stages of the project.

Chalk Sold for setting out a site, chalk lines are intended to be a temporary aid whilst setting out. You could use lime or white cement instead, if you have it. Even inexpensive flour available from all food stores can be used; this is usually the cheapest option for small projects since very little is required.

Squares Indispensable for all aspects of the building operation, both a steel square and an adjustable carpenter's square will be particularly useful. for the projects featured. A home-made wooden square is practical for setting out; it can be made by nailing together three pieces of wood cut in the ratio 3:4:5 - for example, lengths of 0.9 m, 1.2 m and 1.5 m (3 ft, 4 ft and 5 ft) - to create a right-angled corner. A combination square, incorporates a small spirit level, is handy for minor bricklaying projects and carpentry. It also has a 45 degree setting for carpentry work which is useful when marking cutting lines.

Pegs Used for setting out and for holding a builder's line in place, pegs may be metal or wooden, although the latter are cheaper and are also easy to make yourself.

Builder's line Usually fairly strong nylon line, especially manufactured for building (fishing line is quite commonly used), or string is used for setting out, and to ensure that paving or brickwork is straight and level.

Levels Absolutely essential for all stages of any building project, from the foundation up, levels include spirit levels which are available in several lengths, home-made water levels made from transparent tubing (see page 20), and line levels, which can be useful but are not essential.

Punners Ramming tools which you can make by attaching a heavy weight to the end of a pole, punners are useful for smaller jobs and can be used instead of a compacting machine. For larger areas, where earth or hardcore must be compacted before paving or placing concrete, a compacting machine is easier and more efficient. These can usually be hired on a daily basis.

Plumb bobs Used for checking vertical surfaces, a plumb bob is simply a weight attached to a length of string. They are not normally necessary for smaller building projects.

Spades and shovels Used constantly to dig foundations, mix concrete, mortar and plaster on site and place concrete, spades and shovels are mandatory. A pick is also useful for excavating hard ground.

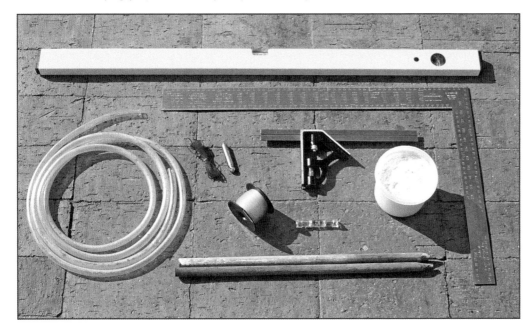

LEFT
Essential tools for setting out and levelling: a spirit level, builder's square, combination square, metal peg and builder's line, transparent tubing, line level and long homemade wooden pegs.

ABOVE RIGHT
A selection of tools used for concrete and brickwork: straightedge marked for checking brick courses (homemade gauge rod), shovel, spade, mortarboard, rubber mallet, wooden corner blocks, pegs and builder's line, bolster (broad chisel), club hammer, wooden float, plasterer's trowel, brick hammer, pointing tool, bricklaying trowel, pointing trowel.

CONCRETE & BRICKWORK

In addition to the basic tools used for levelling and for ensuring that the brickwork is square , level and plumb, there are a number of other items you cannot be without when working with concrete, blocks or bricks.

Wheelbarrows Essential for removing soil from the site and transporting materials, wheelbarrows are useful containers for mixing concrete and mortar. Invest in a good quality builder's wheelbarrow; garden barrows are too shallow to be useful.

Trowels Used for both bricklaying and plastering. Small pointing trowels are useful for neatening the joints of facebrick surfaces, and corner trowels (available for both inner and outer corners) are useful for giving plaster edges a neat finish.

Straightedges and gauge rods are simply straightedged lengths of wood, used to level concrete and to check the mortar joints between brick courses respectively, A gauge rod can easily be made by marking off a straight length of planed-all-round wood at intervals equal to one brick plus a 10 mm (½ in) mortar joint.

Corner blocks are used to string up a builder's line as bricklaying progresses. The line is wrapped around the block and through the slot to secure it, and the blocks are then hooked on to the ends of brickwork. They are also useful for checking

levels and to help you ensure that pillars are square with one another. Metal corner blocks are sometimes available commercially, but they can easily be made by sawing a groove halfway through an L-shaped piece of wood (see photographs on the opposit page).

Pegs and builder's line Used instead of corner blocks, pegs are used with builder's line to identify the upper level of the brick course being laid. Sometimes builders will simply wrap the string around a brick instead.

Hammers Brick hammers that have a distinctive chisel end are often used for cutting bricks. Alternatively, a club hammer may be used with a bolster. A rubber mallet, that looks like a hammer but has a heavy rubber-topped head, is used to tap pavers and slabs into position.

Bolsters Broad chisels or bolsters are useful for cutting bricks neatly.

Jointing tools Although not essential for garden brickwork, various tools are used for pointing or shaping the mortar joints in facebrick walls. A piece of metal may be used instead.

Mortarboards and screedboards Used by professional bricklayers and plasterers respectively to hold small quantities of mortar and plaster while they work.

Floats Made from both wood and metal, floats are used for rendering plaster over bricks and blocks, and the screed used to finish concrete.

WOODWORK

While power tools will simplify just about any carport project, there are some simple hand tools that you cannot afford to be without. You will also need the basic levelling tools, a good quality tape measure and a carpenter's pencil.

Saws The first requirement in any woodwork toolkit., saws come in different shapes and sizes. However careful you are when ordering the correct lengths, of wood there will invariably be some cutting to do. While a stocky back saw or tenon saw will cope with most small jobs, a general purpose bow saw is best for sawing logs, and a hacksaw (which may also be used for cutting metal) is favoured by some do-it-yourselfers. Ripsaws, for cutting along the grain, crosscut saws which work best across the grain, smaller panel saws, which do both, and power saws are all useful.

Drills Although relatively expensive, drills are essential for woodwork. If you do not already own an electric drill (see page 36) and do not intend to invest in one, you could use a hand drill (a wheel brace for minor applications and a more heavy-duty bit brace are both useful) for a relatively simple construction project. Remember that you will also need the correct wood bits for woodwork, and ordinary masonry bits for drilling into brickwork or concrete.

Screwdrivers Indispensable tools, these range from sophisticated spiral ratchet screwdrivers, with different positions and a reverse action, to oridnary screwdrivers with different heads. You will need the right type and size for the job.

Hammers Necessary for nailing pieces of wood together, a claw hammer will also enable you to extract nails.

Spanners are needed to tighten nuts and bolts. There are several types from which to choose.

Chisels, rasps and files are useful for shaping, planing and finishing small lengths of wood, especially when jointing beams.

ABOVE LEFT
A group of four photographs that show how to make a corner block from wood using a tenon saw.

LEFT
A range of tools required for woodwork including a selection of saws, screwdrivers and wood chsels, as well as a retractable steel tape measure, spanners, hand drills, a rap and file, and a claw hammer.

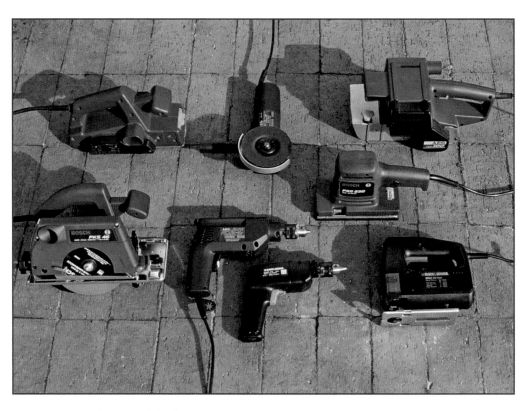

POWER TOOLS

Although power tools are not an essential requirement, there is no doubt that they do take the drudgery out of many jobs. They also enable you to cope with many construction problems which hand tools simply cannot manage.

Drills Designed to simplify most projects, drills are most commonly used for woodwork, but are also indespensible if you are attaching a carport to a wall of some kind. For joining wood, screws are more accurate and will give a more secure grip than nails, but holes must be drilled for them.

Although a single-speed drill is the cheapest option, a two-speed or variable-speed drill is more versatile and therefore undoubtedly a better buy, although it will obviously cost more. An electric drill with a hammer action is useful if you need to drill into really hard materials such as concrete lintels. Cordless drills, which run on batteries, are also available.

Saws Essential for cutting wood, power saws (rather than the saws featured on page 35) will speed up and streamline the job. A circular saw will enable you to make smooth perpendicular or angled cuts in most materials, while a jigsaw will enable you to cut curved lines.

Planers Used to smooth the surface of long pieces of wood at home. (as opposed to buying planed wood), planers may also be used for bevelling or angling edges of lumber and for cutting simple rebates.

Sanders Useful for smoothing timber that has already been planed. A belt sander will remove material quickly and is the best tool to use for levelling planks and boards; vibrating orbital sanders are better for finishing a surface which would otherwise be sanded by hand.

Other useful power tools These include compactors and plate vibrators (which compact hardcore or soil for foundations or paving); angle grinders for cutting bricks and tiles; and block splitters or masonry saws for halving some precast-concrete products.

ABOVE RIGHT
Useful power tools: belt sander, angle grinder, planer, orbital sander, circular saw, two drills, jigsaw.

RIGHT
A compactor being used to compress and stabilize the ground ready for surfacing with pavers, cobblestones or asphalt (tar).

Roofing

Your choice of roof covering will depend on the degree of protection required. Cost will also be a factor, but make sure the chosen material suits the structure you are planning to build.

PLAN FOR HARMONY

If your carport is going to be an extension of your house, the ideal is to use the same roof covering for continuity. However, this is not often practicable, and a different roofing material need not detract from the good looks of a carport. For instance tiles require a pitched roof, and this is not often feasible or desired when building a carport. Glass fiber, fiber-cement or steel sheeting is not only cheaper than tiles, it is also easier to handle and quicker to install.

There are many other ways of achieving harmony, for instance by matching the fascias of the carport to the roof of the house, for example by affixing slate tiles (see plan 5, Slate Sophistication, page 60), or by using the same brick for the piers or pillars that were used for the house or garden walls. Color may also be used to tie the house and carport together.

ELEMENTS OF ROOFING

While a carport roof is not usually as complex a sttructure as either a garage or house roof, it does have certain elements that must be considered. Apart from the roof covering (see pages 39 and 40), there may be beams, fascia board and gutters and downpipes. Flashing may also be used.

Roof Beams A timber-frame roof with wooden beams is the most common structure utilized for carports. Galvanized steel and aluminum may, however, be used instead. It is important to ensure that all the materials can be used in conjunction with each other, if for instance you opt for metal uprights combined with lumber beams. Also, you should make sure that the materials will be aesthetically compatible.

Fascia Board Fascias usually abut guttering along the front of the carport roof, and, once again, the most common material used is wood, either laminated or planed all round. Aluminum, fiber-cement or PVC fascias may also be used.

Gutters and downpipes Although not always considered essential, gutters and downpipes are often used on carport structures to ensure that

ABOVE LEFT
A brick pillared carport using facebricks that match the brickwork style of the house has been covered with a pretty golden shower (Pyrostegia venusta) creeper.

there is effective drainage. Both gutters and downpipes are commonly available in plastic (PVC), fiber-cement, galvanized metal or aluminum; ideally though whatever you use should match up with that utilized for the house and and outbuildings. Gutters are attached to the fascia board with brackets, and downpipes are fitted to the guttering to ensure that rainwater is channeled away from the structure. While most open carports do not incorporate gutters, if there is a solid roof covering, it's best to channel water away from the roof beams.

Flashing The location of your carport, as well as its design, will determine whether flashing of any type is required. Flashing is designed to prevent water from seeping from the roof structure into or down any adjoining walls, and a variety of standard types is available, including flashing made from aluminum or galvanized steel. Numerous fiber and acrylic flashing, as well as paint-on waterproofing products are also available off the shelf. Side-wall and head-wall flashings are used to cover the area where the roof meets a vertical wall, and cover flashing is built into the wall, over the edge of the side- or head-wall flashing, to allow for the expansion and contraction of the roof in changing weather conditions.

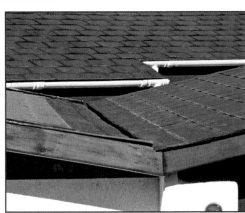

ABOVE LEFT
Guttering is attached to the fascia with brackets.

ABOVE RIGHT
A well sealed drainage channel where sloping roofs meet.

CENTER LEFT
Acrylic and fabric flashing is used to seal the join where the carport roof meets a brick chimney stack.

CENTER RIGHT
Holes are drilled in glass fiber sheeting so that it can be nailed to the purlins of the carport (see pages 43 to 46)

RIGHT
Glass fiber sheeting is a popular choice for carport roofing as it is easy to work with and usually reasonably priced.

COVERINGS

Most carport roofs are fairly flat, sometimes deceptively so, but if the roof covering is solid, there should always be a slight slope for drainage. Usually this slope is not more than three to five degrees (which is a one in twenty to one in ten gradient), and in most cases, it pitches away from the building if the structure is not freestanding.

Plant growth Creepers may be grown over pergola-type carports that do not accommodate a formal covering. With time, some plants may provide adequate protection from the sun's harmful rays. Flowering creepers will also look attractive when in full bloom. Local climatic conditions do have a profound effect on planting, so if you aren't sure of what creepers to use, check with your local nursery.

Shadecloth Numerous grades of shadecloth are available, offering varying degrees of protection from the sun. Shadecloth comes in a number of colors, including green or black. Unless waterproof, it will not protect your car from rain or heavy dew, though it will act as an umbrella in the event of hail. It comes in rolls and can be nailed to a wooden superstructure.

Bituminous felt Like shadecloth, bituminous felt (Malthoid) is bought in roll form. It is black and waterproof and will therefore give protection from both sun and rain. It must be nailed to a wooden roof structure and sealed around the nails with bitumen paste.

Steel sheeting Commonly called corrugated iron, this is either galvanized or color-coated, and it may be cut to size. It is available in a number of profiles, including IBR and S-rib (called 'corrugated' in the trade). Steel sheeting comes in standard widths usually covering up to 762 mm (30 in) and is cut to the lengths required. It is relatively inexpensive, and popular for carports. It may be attached with drive screws (hammered in) or top-speed screws (turned in). When laying steel sheeting (or, indeed, any opaque roofing) stretch a string over the sheeting from one end of a beam to the other, otherwise you may lose track of where the beam is.

Glass fiber Sheets of glass fiber are available in a number of profiles (including corrugated and IBR) and colors (white, green, blue and transparent). Lightweight, and therefore easy to handle, glass fiber sheeting is often pre-drilled, and can be attached to the crossbeams with top-speed screws. It comes in the same standard widths as steel sheeting, but may be more than double the price.

Fiber-cement sheeting Available in a wide selection of profiles, fiber-cement roof sheeting is heavier than other sheeting materials, and sturdier roof trusses and longer fasteners are therefore required. Big Six and Canadian profiles are used most frequently for carports. Standard lengths normally vary from 3,6 m to 7,5 m (11¾ ft to 24½ ft) although this form of sheeting can also be cut to size. It will cover widths from 875 mm to more than a meter (34½ in to 40 in). Profiles vary in price between the prices of steel sheeting and glass fiber. When cutting or drilling fiber-cement products, always follow the manufacturer's safety recommendations.

Polycarbonate sheeting The most modern roof sheeting suitable for carports is made of a strong plastic material called polycarbon. A highly superior - and therefore expensive - material, which the experts say won't crack or fade, it is very smooth, having the visual quality of glass or perspex. It is available in transparent form or colored bronze or opaque white, and in a corrugated, IBR or Big Six profile. It comes in the same standard widths as glass fiber and steel sheeting.

Aluminum Lightweight and therefore easy to handle, aluminum is, ironically perhaps, a form of roof sheeting more frequently installed by professionals. It is available in interlocking sheets of up to 3 m x 6 m (10 ft to 30 ft).

Tiles Any roof tiles may be used for a carport, however because of structural implications, the cost factor inhibits their frequent use. They are particularly useful for people wishing to match up and extend the roof line of the house to incorporate the carport into the overall design.

LEFT
Shadecloth that is waterproofed has been used on this carport to protect from the sun as well as heavy rain, hail and snow.

TOP
An unusual fibre-cement sheet profile.

ABOVE LEFT
Bituminous felt is supplied in rolls and is easily fixed to the roof beams. It is probably the least sophisticated covering available.

ABOVE RIGHT
Coated box-rib steel sheeting will withstand all weather conditions and is protected against rust.

LOWER CENTER LEFT
Polycarbonate sheeting is long-lasting and UV resistant. It allows light into the carport area but reduces the heat.

LOWER CENTER RIGHT
Tiles that match and blend in with the tiles used for the roof of the house have been used for this carport roof.

RIGHT
Shadecloth is an easy covering to install and where available, it comes in various grades and colors.

Parking Surfaces

Although cost is a major consideration in deciding on a ground surface for your carport, it is better to wait until you are able to afford a suitable surface than to settle for second best. An unsuitable surface could provide difficulties at a later stage, and end up costing you more, in the long run, than something more suitable but more expensive.

PLAN FOR HARMONY

In order to create the best aesthetic effect, try to match the materials used for your driveway and your carport ground surface. If you are brick-paving the driveway, pave the entire area; if you've opted for a concrete slab as a parking surface, consider a driveway of concrete strips with grass or a ground cover between them.

EXCAVATION

A structure that is going to last must be built on a firm, solid foundation. If the site is level and the soil stable, minimal excavation followed by compaction of the ground will be sufficient preparation for most parking surfaces.

The base course is the bottom of the excavated area, onto which the ground surface for the carport is built. The most important consideration with any base course is that it should be firm, level and well compacted. If the soil is clay, it will probably be necessary to dig a 300-mm (1 ft) foundation and fill this with a mixture generally known as hardcore, which is made up of broken bricks, rubble, stones and other hard material. It may also be a good idea to prepare a hardcore base and compact this well if the soil is very soft or sandy. Gaps in the hardcore should be filled with sand, in order to provide a level area on which to lay your surface material. Tarmac can be laid on ash.

DRAINAGE

If you are building away from the house on stable, level ground, and you do not intend to construct a solid roof, drainage will not be an issue. Nevertheless, the matter of drainage should never be overlooked. If rainwater is allowed to accumulate, you could find yourself with an unusable quagmire in wet weather.

RETAINING WALLS

Remember that retaining walls may be necessary whenever there is a steep change in level where your carport meets the rest of the garden area, in order to prevent earth and rocks from falling

ABOVE LEFT
A herringbone patterned driveway leads to a carport.

FAR LEFT
A slate-tiled, crazy paving area under the carport structure blends in with the house.

LEFT
Asphalt is a good firm surface for driveways and carports, even though it is not the most aesthetically pleasing surface available. It's a good budget option.

ABOVE TOP
Cobblestones are ideal for carport surfaces and driveways.

ABOVE CENTER
Regular cut slate is attractive and hardwearing.

ABOVE BOTTOM
Granite crushed stone or gravel is inexpensive and may be used until you can afford what you really want.

RIGHT
A concrete slab floated to form a nice smooth surface under a shadecloth-covered carport.

onto the carport ground surface. Leave a space of 150 mm (6 in) between the wall and the ground around the carport, and dig a trench in the gap. Fill with crushed stone or gravel for drainage. It may sometimes be necessary to leave drainage holes in your retaining wall. The simplest way of doing this is to leave quarter-brick-wide gaps, approximately a meter apart, in the second course of bricks in the wall.

THE RANGE OF SURFACES

Mother earth Perhaps the most common and yet most inefficient carport surface is bare earth. If the ground is firm and you do not live in a high-rainfall area, it may be acceptable. However, for both aesthetic and practical reasons, it is recommended that other options be considered. If, for some reason, you do not have a choice, it is advisable to compact the ground to form a solid base.

Gravel Crushed stone of mixed sizes makes an inexpensive and acceptable parking surface, but it should be well compacted to give your car tyres a good grip. Ask for gravel or crushed stone suitable for a base course, and not the 'single-sized' stone used for concrete mixes, as these may cause your car tyres to slip. Stone used for gravel varies in different parts of the world, but includes granite, sandstone and laterite.

Railway sleepers A popular material for the garden, wooden sleepers may be embedded in the soil to form a fairly hardy parking surface, although their use on a sloping surface is not recommended, as they become slippery when wet. They should be laid level with the ground surface, and gaps between them should be filled with earth. They may also be used in combination with concrete or bricks. In many areas sleepers are in short supply, but check the classified section of your online directory or local newspaper. Sometimes nurseries stock them.

Concrete paving slabs When laying precast-concrete paving slabs, make sure that the slabs are level with each other, otherwise vehicles driving over the surface will exert uneven stress, and cause them to become loose and unstable. To lay them, excavate to 100 mm (4 in), compact the earth, then lay the slabs on 40 to 50 mm (1 ½ to 2 in) of builder's sand. Overall cost is much the same as for a single slab of concrete.

Concrete slab A single concrete slab is a common parking surface that is easily laid by the amateur builder (*see pages 47 to 50*). If you plan to enclose the carport at a later date to form a garage, extra care should be taken to ensure that you have a smooth level concrete base in order to simplify future building. To avoid cracking, throw no more than nine square meters (100 ft²) at a time. This will allow for the expansion and contraction of the concrete caused by changes in temperature.

Regular-cut slate and crazy paving Irregular or crazy paving may be used for patios, driveways and domestic parking surfaces. It consists of pieces of randomly shaped slate laid in a concrete base. Slate cut into regular shapes may also be laid in newly placed concrete.

Asphalt Also called Tarmac (short for Tarmacadam), asphalt is a mixture of crushed stone and bitumen. It is usually applied hot, and special equipment will have to be hired for this. It is probably the cheapest solid parking surface available and is quick to lay; though it should ideally be applied by a specialist.

Brick paving This is a versatile surface, as both clay and concrete bricks come in a variety of colors. These can be laid in a number of different ways to create different patterns (see page 51). Brick paving has the advantage of being able to take huge loads – some paving companies will guarantee the paving to take loads of up to 4 000 kg (4 tons). The quality of brick chosen will affect the price of the paving.

Interlocking road stones Shaped, concrete paving bricks and interlocking road stones are practical alternatives to brick paving. They are manufactured in various colors and cost much the same as regular concrete pavers. The same laying procedure applies as for concrete paving blocks.

Cobblestones Manufatured from concrete, cobblestones are made to mimic old-fashioned roadstones. They are not a flat as regular pavers, but may be used to create an attractive parking surface.

Pebble paving Not universally available, this involves a process in which river stones or pebbles are bonded together in a special resin-and-concrete mixture and then laid to form a continuous surface about 13 mm (½ in) thick. It is applied over concrete, but is not recommended as a do-yourself project. It is attractive and practical though fairly pricey.

CHAPTER FOUR
Build a Carport Step-by-Step

CARPORT STEP-BY-STEP

For a carport to offer maximum shelter, it must have a solid roof covering, and uprights must be sturdy to support a reasonably substantial roof structure.

MATERIALS

Pillars can be built of bricks or blocks; here, 390 mm x 190 mm x 190 mm (15 in x 7½ in x 7½ in) hollow concrete blocks were used. The front pillars are 2.4 m (8 ft) high, with 26 blocks in each. The back two are one block higher (28 in each) to give a 1:25 slope to the roof. You will also need concrete for the footings and mortar and plaster for the pillars. You will find a guide to proportions and quantities on pages 16 and 21.

Cut and planed timber is a common choice for the roof structure. The timber dimensions depend on the size of the carport - this one is 6 m x 3.5 m (20 ft x 11 ft 9 in). The roof structure is made of standard planed timber. Beams are 6.6 m (21 fl 6 in) long and 231 mm x 69 mm (9 in x 2¾ in) in section. The seven purlins are 3.6 m (11 ft 9 in) long and 144 mm x 44 mm (5½ in x 1¾ in) across. You will also need scrap timber to brace the beams while installing the roof structure. Glass fiber sheeting covers the roof structure.

Galvanized strapping for fastening the beams is concreted into the pillars as you work on the final two courses. Purlins are attached to the beams with truss hangers that are secured with coach screws and hexagonal bolts; roof sheeting is attached with roofing screws. PVC guttering and a downpipe complete the design.

1. Set out the site (see page 23), ensuring that the layout is square. Dig four 800 mm x 800 mm (2 ft 8 in x 2 ft 8 in) foundation footings at least 400 mm (1 ft 4 in) deep. Knock a peg into the centre of each to indicate the upper level of the concrete to be placed..

2. Pour the concrete mixture into each hole to the height of the peg. Allow to set overnight. At the outer corner of each pillar, set up a profile by knocking a batten or similar piece of wood into the ground. Check that it is plumb with the planned block surface.

3. Using corner blocks, set up a line between two of the profiles. Position the first course of blocks without mortar and use a steel square to check the angles. Mark off the upright timber to form a gauge rod that shows one course plus a 10 mm (¾ in) mortar joint.

4. Starting about 1 m (3 ft) from the ground, mark off a gauge on each of the other three profiles, using a water level (see page 20) to ensure that the blockwork will be level. If you are working alone, use tape to hold the water level to the profiles.

5. Mix mortar as described on page 26 and then, using a trowel, place a small amount on top of the concrete foundation - enough to place the block on to. Now lay the first block, pushing it firmly into the mortar, levelling it with the first line marked on your gauge rod.

6. Lay two blocks side by side, alternating the direction for each course. Put mortar onto the surface of the block, then tap the next one into place with handle of the trowel. Keep checking both horizontal and vertical surfaces with a spirit level as you work

7. When you have laid about six courses, fill in the holes in the blocks with a weak concrete mix. If you are building brick pillars, use metal reinforcing to strengthen the structure. This is held in place with concrete or mortar which fills the central cavity.

8. Continue laying until the pillar is about 2.4 m (7 ft 9 in) high. Insert galvanized strapping or hoop iron into one of the holes of the final two courses (preferably place them at the outermost corner), and fill up the cavities in the blocks with concrete as before.

9. You can plaster (render) the pillars now or once the roof structure has been assembled (see page 25). Using a combination square, measure and mark the positions of the seven purlins on the two side beams; this is where you will attach the truss hangers for the cross beams.

10. Still working on the ground, mark the position of the coach screws on the beams and drill holes at these points. Ensure that the truss hangers are accurately positioned, then fix to the timber. Use a spanner or ratchet to tighten the screws; do not over tighten.

11. When the mortar in the pillars is completely dry, place the beams across them. Brace with battens, ensuring that the distance between them is constant and that they are level and plumb. Hammer the strapping to fit over the beams and nail it down.

12. Carefully lower the purlins into position. If your measuring has been accurate, you will not have any problems, and the timber crosspieces will slot in quite easily. If necessary you can hammer the ends gently to force them snugly into the truss hangers.

13. Check that each of the purlins is level. If any of them seem to sag or are slightly lower on one side, wedge a piece of wood between the timber and the truss hanger until they are level. This is absolutely essential for the roof sheeting to be laid flat and evenly.

14. Place the roof sheeting on the purlins and drill holes in the upper section of the glass fiber profile where it covers the timber. If a join is required, overlap the sheeting. Hammer 65 mm (2½ in) roofing screws into each hole to secure the sheeting. do not hammer too deep

15. The slope you have created will ensure that rainwater drains off the structure towards the gutter, which is fixed to the lowest purlin with brackets and clout nails. Connect the gutter to the downpipe with an outlet fitting and use swan necks to angle it.

16. Finish off with a good quality paint. There are numerous types of paint from which to choose, although the most usual kind found on rendered brick outdoor structures is a good quality water-based paint. Gloss paints are often used on the wood; most require an undercoat.

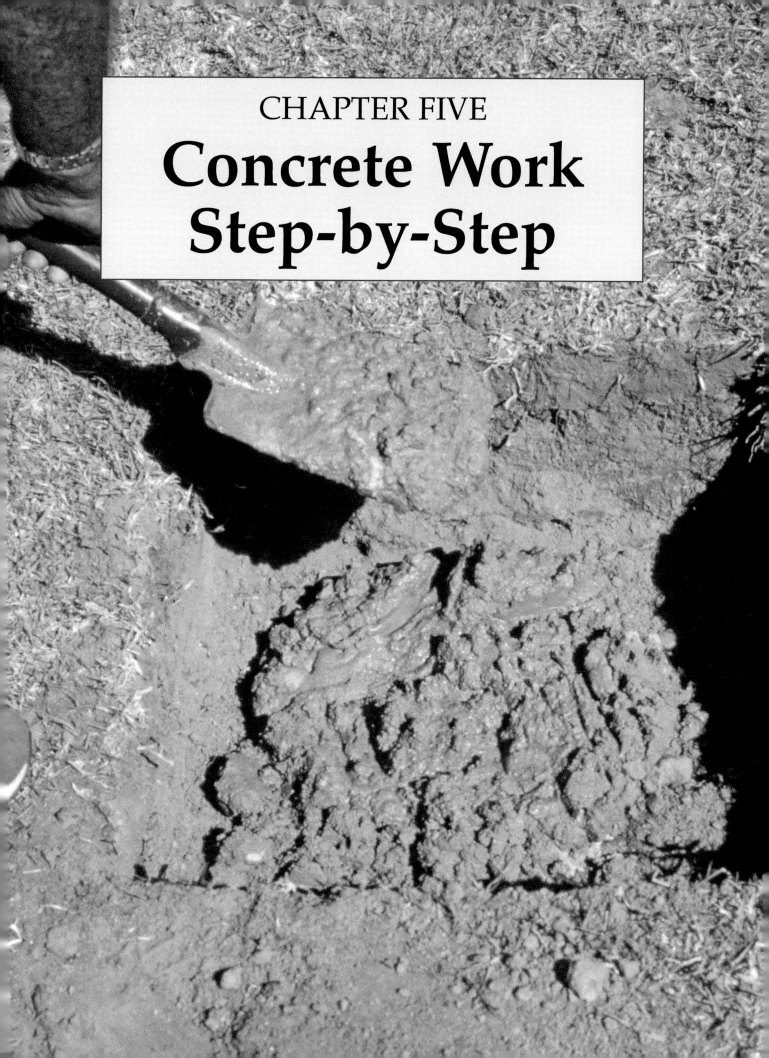

CHAPTER FIVE
Concrete Work Step-by-Step

CONCRETE STEP-BY-STEP

The principles of casting or placing concrete are the same for foundations, footings and solid slabs. When you tackle a large area, the concrete should be cast in sections of up to 9 m² (97 ft²); place alternate sections one day and the rest when the concrete has set.

MATERIALS

A basic concrete mix consists of cement, sand, stone and water. The quantities and ratio you use depend on the area to be covered and how heavy the traffic using the surface will be as this will dictate the ratios to be mixed (see pages 16 and 20 to 22). The concrete slab of a carport floor should be at least 100 mm (4 in) thick so that it can carry the weight without cracking.

CONSTRUCTION

Formwork or shuttering You will need to create formwork or shuttering to contain the concrete while it sets and hardens.

Use timber or metal (preferably aluminum) forms, lightly oiled with a proprietary release agent to prevent the concrete from sticking to them. Set out the area to be concreted as shown on page 23, with additional pegs around the edge, about 1 m (3 ft) apart. Then set up formwork to a height corresponding to the required depth of the slab.

Cracks If cracks develop in the slab while the concrete is still malleable, the surface can be reworked within four hours of pouring (before it sets). To repair cracks in old concrete, chip away loose material, coat the cracks with a bonding agent and patch with new concrete.

1. Start by preparing the site. Dig out the soil to a depth of about 150 mm (6 in) - or 100 mm (4 in) if hardcore is not needed - making sure that the ground is firm and level so that the concrete will settle evenly. Remove all vegetation, including roots.

2. Hardcore, or crushed stone, will provide a more stable base on a site with loose or clay soil. It may also be used to fill any holes. Measure the area for the carport and spread the material evenly with a shovel to form a 50 mm (2 in) thick sub-base.

3. Level the surface as best you can. Fill any gaps in the sub-base with clean builder's sand and compact it thoroughly with a punner. Alternatively, specialised equipment such as a compactor or plate vibrator may be hired to simplify the job.

4. Check the level you have created using a spirit level, placed on a straightedge if necessary. You will need to allow a slight gradient of about 1:40 away from any adjacent building in order to provide effective drainage of rainwater towards the trench.

5. Before you fix the formwork in place, divide the area into sections which are no more than 9 m² (97 ft²) in size. When the formwork is removed, you will be left with joints which will help prevent uncontrolled and unsightly cracking of the concrete.

6. Hammer wooden or metal pegs into the ground where you want the corners of each section to be. String a builder's line between them, 100 mm (4 in) above the sub-base, to mark the intended finished height of the concrete surface.

7. Now you can set up the formwork, ensuring that the top of each length corresponds with the line. Hammer pegs into the ground on either side of the formwork to keep it in place. If necessary, place wedges under the lengths to raise them.

8. Keep checking the levels of the formwork with a spirit level as you go, once again allowing for a slight drainage slope. The formwork must be set accurately at this stage as its top edge will determine the final finished surface level of the concrete slab.

9. You will need a clean, dry container to measure out the required quantities of cement, sand and stone. It should be strong hardwearing and rigid; a 12 litre (2½ gal) builder's bucket, an empty 25 litre (5½ gal) paint can, or a large oil drum is ideal.

10. If you are using a concrete mixer, load the stone first, together with a little water. Add the cement next and then the sand, with just enough water to make the mixture workable. If you are mixing by hand, first mix the cement and sand and then add the stone last.

11. Before pouring the concrete, moisten the ground first to prevent the sub-base and soil from drawing water out from the mixture. Transport the concrete to the site in a wheelbarrow and start to pour it into the section of formwork furthest from your mixing place.

12. Overfill the formwork so that the concrete is about 25 mm (1 in) above it before compaction. Use a chopping action with a straightedge or heavy wooden beam to compact the wet concrete and expel all air. Use a sawing motion to level it.

13. Care must be taken to work the concrete against the formwork and into all corners. If there are any hollows or gaps, these should be filled and levelled. The concrete is sufficiently compact when pasty cement and water starts to come to the surface.

14. Finish the surface with a float, pressing down and using a circular movement. Since the outdoor concrete finish should be fairly rough if it is not to become slippery in wet weather, then use a wooden float to do this. A steel float will create a very smooth finish.

15. A jointing tool should be used to avoid any unsightly cracks appearing across your finished slab. The joints allow any shrinking cracks that happen when the concrete dries out to only occur where the tool has been used. Here a piece of flat bar does the job.

16. In moderate climates, formwork can usually be removed the day after the concrete is cast. Ideally, allow it to cure for five to seven days. Either cover the surface with plastic or sacking (which should be kept damp), or gently hose it down regularly.

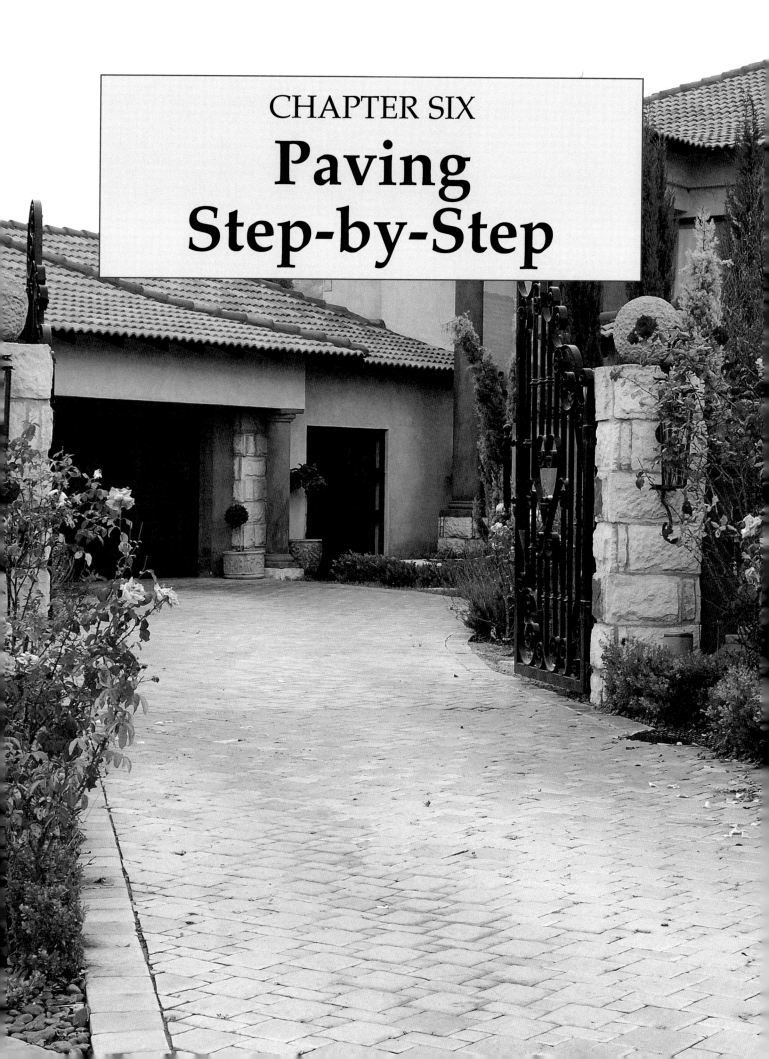

CHAPTER SIX
Paving Step-by-Step

PAVING STEP-BY-STEP

Brick paving is one of the most popular floor surfaces for patios and carports, and it is a project which all do-it-yourselfers can easily undertake. Although paving is sometimes laid on concrete, it is frequently simply placed on a bed of sand. If you have unstable soil (such as clay), incorporate a well-compacted base of hardcore beneath the surface.

MATERIALS

The type of brick you use will depend largely on the effect you wish to create. Clay and concrete bricks or blocks are available in several colors and can be laid in various patterns. Lay the bricks on clean builder's sand, 25-50 mm (1-2 in) thick, depending on the site.

1. Measure the area and set out with pegs and line to define the space for the carport floor. Excavate the site to the correct depth, removing all vegetation. Make sure that the base is stable and well compacted. Spread fill or soil to level the site.

3. Lay 150 micron plastic sheeting over the levelled surface, overlapping the edges by about 150 mm (6 in). This will act as a damp-proof course and will also prevent weeds and grass from growing through gaps between the paving bricks or blocks.

CONSTRUCTION

Edging Some sort of edging, firmly bedded in mortar, should hold the outer edges of paving in place. Precast-concrete kerbstones work well along the borders of any paved surface to be used by cars, especially if a carport is built on a street boundary.

Bricks are reasonably common around the edges of a carport floor or driveway. They can be laid to form a soldier, sailor or header course. Alternatively, strips of timber may be used, or you can erect a narrow formwork around the edge and pour in a weak concrete mix, take care to work cleanly and keep your paving clean. It is best to start paving at one edge, but do not lay all the edges at once or you may end up with an odd-shaped space which will cause unnecessary cutting of bricks.

2. In some instances it may be necessary to include a hardcore sub-base. Both this and any fill must be thoroughly compacted to prevent future subsidence. You can use a punner, although it is more efficient to use a compacting machine that can be hired.

4. Spread 30-50 mm (1-2 in) of clean builder's sand evenly over the plastic. Although river sand is often quite clean, it is advisable not to use unwashed beach, dune or pit sand as these tend to contain salt, shell particles or excessive amounts of clay.

5. Smooth the sand by drawing a straightedge evenly across it. Keep checking your levels as you work with a spirit level placed on top of the straightedge to ensure that there is a 1:40 gradient. This will allow for drainage away from any adjacent buildings.

6. If the paving is to abut a wall, start laying from this point; alternatively, begin at an edging (see page 52). Work systematically inwards, using a builder's square from time to time to ensure that the pattern is square and even. A builder's line can also help keep your laying line straight.

7. Press the pavers into the sand to create the design of your choice (in this series of pictures, basketweave). Unless you want a mortar joint, abut the bricks and gently tap each one into position with a rubber mallet. Use a spirit level to check that they are level.

8. If any brick is below the level of the paving, lift it out and pack a little extra sand in underneath where it is needed. Replace the brick and tap it with the mallet to bed it into place. If a brick is too high, remove some of the sand before putting it back in place.

9. Inevitably there will be bricks which have to be cut. You can do this by scoring a clean cutting line on all four sides with a bolster, then hitting the tool with a club hammer to break it. Alternatively, you can use the chisel end of a brick hammer.

10. Once you have laid all the pavers, check the levels again. If any of the bricks protrude slightly, lay a straight plank across the surface and hammer with the mallet to flatten them. Do not hammer the bricks themselves or you may dislodge or damage them.

11. To fill any slight gaps between the pavers, sweep a dry and weak 1:6 cement:sand mixture over the surface with a stiff bristled brush. Although sand alone may be used, the cement will improve bonding and help to ensure that all the bricks stay in place.

12. Use a garden hose to finely spray the entire area lightly with clean water. If any mortar remains on the surface, gently squeegee the bricks to remove it. Allow the cement to set thoroughly - for at least 48 hours - before driving on the paving.

BRICK PAVING PATTERNS

Herringbone

Basketweave

Half Basketweave

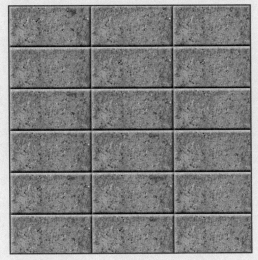

Jack-On-Jack

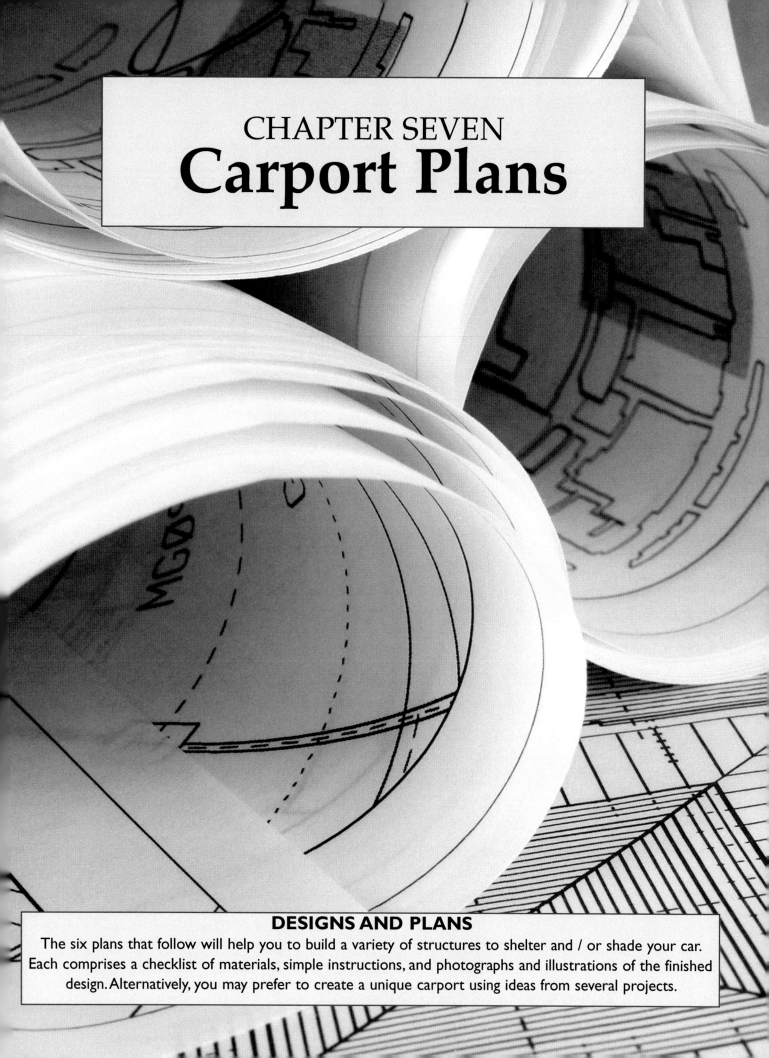

CHAPTER SEVEN
Carport Plans

DESIGNS AND PLANS

The six plans that follow will help you to build a variety of structures to shelter and / or shade your car. Each comprises a checklist of materials, simple instructions, and photographs and illustrations of the finished design. Alternatively, you may prefer to create a unique carport using ideas from several projects.

Plan 1: Wood on Wood

Wooden poles combine with planed timber to create an attractive, free-standing carport which will suit a range of homes and add character to the surrounding garden. The glass fiber roof gives protection from sun, rain and snow.

MATERIALS

Foundations for poles
115 kg (254 lb) cement
465 kg or 0.35 m³ (1,025 lb or 12½ ft³) sand
465 kg or 0.35 m³ (1,025 lb or 12½ ft³) stone

Framework
4 x 3 m (10 ft) upright poles, 100 mm (4 in) in diameter
2 x 7 m x 228 mm x 50 mm (23 ft x 9 in x 2 in) beams
6 x 3.8 m x 75 mm x 50 mm (12 ft 6 in x 3 in x 2 in) purlins
2 x 3.8 m x 114 mm x 32 mm (12 ft 6 in x 4½ in x 1¼ in) fascia boards
8 x 75 mm x 50 mm x 50 mm (3 in x 2 in x 2 in) timber blocks

Roofing
glass fiber sheets to cover 21 m² (225 ft²)

Guttering
1 x 3 m (10 ft) PVC gutter with round channel
1 x 2.5 m (8 ft 3 in) PVC downpipe
1 gutter outlet
6 gutter brackets
2 stop ends
2 downpipe brackets
1 downpipe shoe
2 swan necks
clout nails or screws

Fasteners
8 x 12 mm (½ in) cuphead bolts with nuts and washers
40 x 8 mm (¼ in) coach screws
clout nails
roofing screws

Paving
945 bricks/blocks
1,215 kg or 0.9 m³ (2,678 lb or 32 ft³) sand

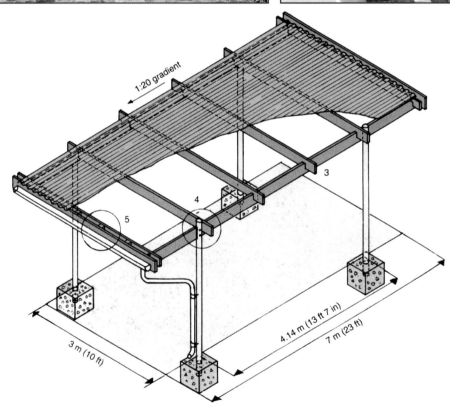

1. Dig four foundations, 500 mm x 500 mm x 500 mm (1 ft 8 in x 1 ft 8 in x 1 ft 8 in) set out as illustrated.
2. Brace poles in position, ensuring that the two back ones are slightly higher for drainage. Pour concrete into holes.
3. Saw out six notches 50 mm (2 in) wide and about 60 mm (2⅜ in) deep at 1.37 m (4 ft 5 in) intervals along both beams. Cut first and last notches 50 mm (2 in) in from ends of each beam.
4. Secure beams to the poles with cuphead bolts (see detail photograph). Slot purlins into the notches, then nail down.
5. Line up four wooden blocks with the ends of beams and attach to the outside of each end purlin with coach screws (see detail photograph). Screw the fascia boards to the blocks and beam ends.
6. Fix roof sheeting to the structure with roofing screws.
7. Attach the gutter and downpipe to the front of the carport.
8. Pave the parking area.

Plan 2: Popular Precast

Six precast concrete pillars form the basis of this attractive yet simple and inexpensive carport. For stability, the pillars are concreted into the ground and three crossbeams are secured with hoop iron. Corrugated glass fiber sheeting, fixed at a slight slope, is used as a roof covering. A gutter is attached along one side, and a downpipe is secured to a short pole which is sunk into the ground.

MATERIALS

Foundations (if necessary)
40 kg (88 lb) cement
160 kg (350 lb) sand
160 kg (350 lb) stone

Framework
6 x 2.1 m (7 ft) precast pillars
3 x 3.3 m x 165 mm x 60 mm
     (11 ft 6½ in x 2⅜ in) beams
5 x 4.64 m x 68 mm x 45 mm
     (15 ft x 2½ in x 1¾ in) purlins
2 x 4.64 m x 170 mm x 20 mm
     (15 ft x 6½ in x ¾ in) fascia
     boards
2 x 3.3 m x 210 mm x 20 mm
     (11 ft x 8 in x ¾ in) fascia boards

Roofing
glass fiber sheets to cover
     15.3 m² (166 ft²)

Guttering
1 x 4.5 m (14 ft 9 in) PVC gutter;
     square channel
1 x 2 m (6 ft 6 in) PVC downpipe
1 x 2.5 m (8 ft) pole
1 gutter outlet
4 gutter brackets
2 stop ends
2 downpipe brackets
1 downpipe shoe

Fasteners
8 mm (¼ in) coach screws
5 m (16 ft 6 in) galvanized strapping
     or hoop iron
roofing screws
clout nails or screws

Paving
690 bricks/blocks
810 kg or 0.6 m³ (1,786 lb or
     22 ft³) sand

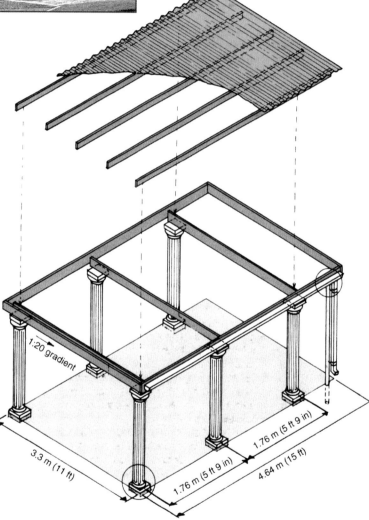

1:20 gradient

3.3 m (11 ft)

1.76 m (5 ft 9 in)

1.76 m (5 ft 9 in)

4.64 m (15 ft)

1. Level the area, allowing for a slight drainage slope across the width of the carport.
2. If the area is already paved or concreted, simply stand pillars on some mortar as indicated. Otherwise, prepare a shallow foundation and set pillars in place on a bed of mortar (see detail photograph).
3. Concrete the strapping into the centre of each pillar. Allow to set before placing the three beams across tops of pillars. Secure with strapping.

4. Skew-nail purlins across beams at intervals of 825 mm (2 ft 9 in).
5. Fix fascia board to all sides with coach screws.
6. Fix roof sheeting in place with roofing screws.
7. Attach the gutter to the back fascia board with brackets (see detail photograph).
8. Set the pole in the ground at rear left-hand corner of structure. Secure downpipe to it with clout nails or screws.
9. Pave the carport floor.

Plan 3: Carport for Shade

This inexpensive all-wood structure is a perfect project for the keen amateur carpenter who needs a shady place for a car. It can be erected in just a few hours. Shadecloth nailed to the simple roof structure protects the car from the sun, snow and hail, although any other suitable awning fabric could be substituted. An attractive planter on one side doubles as a protective wall alongside the sidewalk.

MATERIALS

Foundations for timber uprights
300 kg (660 lb) cement
1,215 kg or 0.9 m³ (2,678 lb or 32 ft³) sand
1,215 kg or 0.9 m³ (2,678 lb or 32 ft³) stone

Foundations for planter
40 kg (88 lb) cement
124 kg (273 lb) or 0.1 m³ (3 ft³) sand
162kg (357 lb) or 0.1 m³ (3 ft³) stone

Framework
12 x 2.45 m x 93 mm x 22 mm (8 ft x 3½ in x 1 in) upright timbers
2 x 6 m x 152 mm x 50 mm (20 ft x 6 in x 2 in) side beams
2 x 3.82 m x 152 mm x 50 mm (12 ft 6 in x 6 in x 2 in) crossbeams
3 x 3.72 m x 118 mm x 38 mm (12ft 2 in x 4½ in x 1½ in) purlins
4 x 3 m x 38 mm x 38 mm (10 ft x 1½ in x 1½ in) battens
6 x 1 m x 93 mm x 50 mm (3 ft 3 in x 3½ in x 2 in) timber spacers
6 x 150 mm x 93 mm x 50 mm (6 in x 3½ in x 2 in) timber spacer blocks

Planter
700 bricks
275 kg (606 lb) cement
1,114 kg or 0.8 m³ (2,456 lb or 28 ft³) plaster sand

Roof covering
shadecloth or awning fabric to cover 23 m² (250 ft²)

Fasteners
18 x 12 mm (½ in) cuphead bolts with nuts and washers
20 x 8 mm (¼ in) coach screws
10 x 12 mm (½ in) coach screws
heavy duty staples or clout nails
wire nails

Paving
1,035 bricks/blocks
0.9 m³ (32 ft³) sand

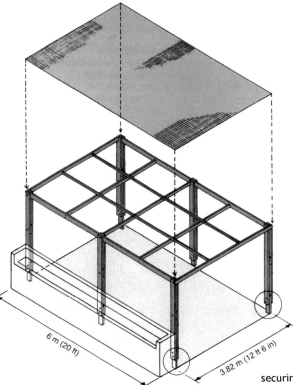
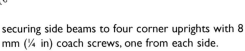

1. The planter can be built before the carport. Dig a foundation 100 mm (4 in) deep, 6.4 m (21 ft) long and 600 mm (2 ft) wide. Pour the concrete. Build halfbrick walls, leaving outer wall two courses lower than inner wall. Plaster or render the surface.

2. Dig six foundations, 600 mm x 600 mm x 600 mm (2 ft x 2 ft x 2 ft).

3. Place the concrete. Push the long spacers into the fresh concrete and allow it to set.

4. Bolt uprights together in pairs with the smaller spacers placed halfway up. Slot over the blocks set in concrete and secure each with two cuphead bolts (see detail photographs).

5. Now begin assembling the roof structure, securing side beams to four corner uprights with 8 mm (¼ in) coach screws, one from each side.

6. Cut about 45 mm (1¾ in) off a purlin, to fit the structure, and attach 38 mm (1½ in) below top of middle pairs of uprights with 12 mm (½ in) coach screws.

7. Nail crossbeams to front and back of the structure.

8. Slot the two remaining purlins into place, halfway between central purlin and crossbeams. Secure as before, using 12 mm (½ in) coach screws.

9. Nail battens into place, skew-nailing where they join above middle purlin.

10. Staple or nail shadecloth or awning fabric to timbers.

11. Pave the carport surface.

Plan 4: Simply Single

This single carport will suit many house styles. It is a solid yet simple structure, designed to fit in front of an existing garage, although it could be freestanding if two more metal poles were used. The roof slopes slightly, away from the existing building, and a concealed gutter is attached to a downpipe that leads to a rainwater channel. In very windy areas you should use thicker poles than those specified.

MATERIALS
Foundations for poles
100 kg (220 lb) cement
405 kg or 0.3 m³ (893 lb or 11 ft³) sand
405 kg or 0.3 m³ (893 lb or 11 ft³) stone

Concrete floor
500 kg (1,100 lb) cement
0.75 m³ (26 ft³) sand
1.2 m³ (42 ft³) stone

Framework
2 metal poles, 76 mm (3 in) in diameter, with support brackets
2 x 5 m x 152 mm x 76 mm (16 ft 5 in x 6 in x 3 in) beams
1 x 3 m x 152 mm x 76 mm (10 ft x 6 in x 3 in) beam.
4 x 3 m x 114 mm x 50 mm (10 ft x 4½ in x 2 in) rafters
1 x 3 m x 76 mm x 50 mm (10 ft x 3 in x 2 in) purlin
2 x 5.1 m x 152 mm x 38 mm (16 ft 9 in x 6 in x 1½ in) fascia boards
1 x 3.3 m x 152 mm x 38 mm (10 ft 10 in x 6 in x 1½ in) fascia

Roofing
glass fiber sheets to cover 15 m² (162 ft²)

Guttering
1 x 3 m (10 ft) PVC gutter with round channel
1 x 2.5 m (8 ft 3 in) PVC downpipe
1 gutter outlet
4 gutter brackets
2 stop ends
2 downpipe brackets
1 downpipe shoe
2 swan necks
clout nails or screws
precast rainwater channel (optional)

Fasteners
4 x 12 mm (½ in) Rawl bolts
10 x 100 mm x 50 mm x 50 mm (4 in x 2 in x 2 in) galvanized angle brackets, 3 mm (⅛ in) thick
53 x 8 mm (¼ in) coach screws
clout nails
6 x 4.5 mm (³⁄₁₆ in) self-tapping screws
roofing screws

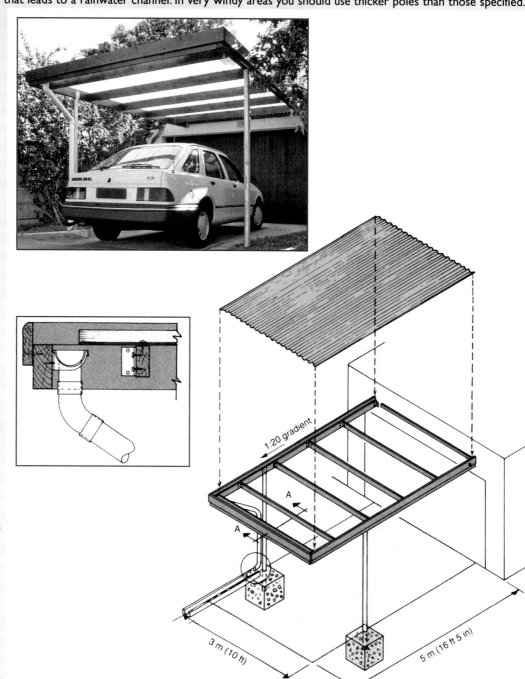

1. Dig two foundations, 600 mm x 600 mm x 600 mm (2 ft x 2 ft x 2 ft).
2. Set poles in concrete, brace and allow concrete to set.
3. Cast the concrete slab, either now or when the structure is complete.
4. Fix the purlin to wall with angle brackets and Rawl bolts, allowing for a slight drainage slope.
5. Using coach screws, attach the longer beams to the angle brackets and to the support brackets at tops of the poles. Then attach the shorter beam between the side beams at the front of the structure.
6. Working from the back of the structure, attach rafters to beams, fixing an angle bracket to each side of the rafter at both ends for added stability.
7. Nail gutter brackets to inside surface of front beam and attach gutter (see detail sketch).
8. Screw fascia boards to structure on all three sides, concealing guttering.
9. Fix the roof sheeting to structure with roofing screws.

Plan 5: Slate Sophistication

This double carport was designed to be attached to the front of a garage. Its framework consists of two brick pillars with a wooden roof structure bolted on to the garage wall. Corrugated iron sheeting has been used for protection, while guttering is concealed between the wall and the carport. The look has been enhanced by fixing slate tiles to the beams to match the roof of the house.

MATERIALS

Foundations for pillars
90 kg (200 lb) cement
365 kg or 0.3 m³ (805 lb or 11 ft³)
 sand
365 kg or 0.3 m³ (805 lb or 11 ft³)
 stone

Framework
360 facebricks
90 kg (200 lb) cement
50 kg (112 lb) lime
365 kg or 0.3 m³ (805 lb or 11 ft³)
 sand extra cement, sand and
 stone for concrete to fill pillar
 cavity
2 x 2.4 m (8 ft) reinforcing rods
2 x 6 m x 297 mm x 50 mm
 (20 ft x 12 in x 2 in) beams
4 x 6.2 m 297 mm x 70 mm
 (20 ft 4 in x 12 in x 2½ in) rafters

Roofing
corrugated iron sheeting to cover
 38 m² (410 ft²)
72 x 350 mm x 260 mm
 (1 ft 2 in x 10 in) slate tiles

Guttering
1 x 6.2 m (20 ft 4 in) PVC gutter
 with square channel
1 x 2 m (6 ft 6 in) PVC downpipe
1 gutter outlet
5 gutter brackets
2 stop ends
2 downpipe brackets
1 downpipe shoe
clout nails or screws
precast concrete channel

Fasteners
8 x 200 mm x 80 mm x 80 mm
 (8 in x 3 in x 3 in) galvanizedd
 angle brackets, 3 mm (⅛ in) thick
50 x 8 mm (¼ in) coach screws
2 wall plates
10 anchor bolts
clout nails
roofing screws
hoop iron

Paving
1,512 bricks/blocks
1.3 m³ (46 ft³) sand

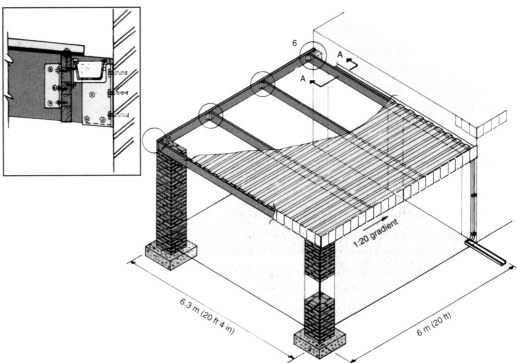

1. Dig two foundations, 800 mm x 800 mm x 300 mm (2 ft 8 in x 2 ft 8 in x 12 in).
2. Place concrete into the footings and leave to set overnight.
3. Build pillars to a height of 2.4 m (8 ft), building hoop iron into the centre for last five courses. Allow mortar to set thoroughly.
4. Bolt wall plates to the wall opposite the pillars, but slightly lower to allow for a drainage slope.
5. Screw angle brackets onto the beams at equal intervals, leaving a gap at one end for concealed gutter. Fix beams in place so that they extend over outer edges of pillars, securing with the hoop iron that you embedded in the pillars.
6. Attach the guttering to one of the rafters and fix between the beams (see detail illustration and photograph).
7. Working away from the wall, position the rafters and screw in place.
8. Fix roof sheeting to the structure with roofing screws.
9. Use clout nails to fix tiles to outside of exposed beams.
10. Pave the parking area.

Plan 6: Clever Combination

With good planning, a carport can double as a storage area for garden tools. This brick structure incorporates a small, windowless shed at one end, behind the carport wall. A low wall is included in the design because the site slopes, although for flat sites this would not be necessary. While a knowledge of bricklaying is required for this project, you do not have to be a professional to tackle it.

MATERIALS

Foundations for pillars and walls (including storeroom)
700 kg (1,550 lb) cement
2.1 m³ (73 ft³) sand
2.1 m³ (73 ft³) stone

Brickwork
5,250 bricks
2,000 kg (4,409 lb) cement
2 m³ (70 ft³) plaster sand
extra cement, sand and stone to fill cavity in pillars
4 x 2.4 m (8 ft) reinforcing rods
2 airbricks

Roof structure
2 x 7.8 m x 278 mm x 50 mm (25 ft 6 in x 11 in x 2 in) beams
6 x 6 m x 278 mm x 50 mm (20 ft x 11 in x 2 in) purlins
2 x 7.8 m x 278 mm x 30 mm (25 ft 6 in x 11 in x 1 in) fascia boards
1 x 6 m x 278 mm x 30 mm (20 ft x 11 in x 1 in) fascia board

Roofing
corrugated steel sheeting to cover 36 m² and 5.64 m² (390 ft² and 60 ft²)
glass fiber sheeting with matching corrugation to cover 5.64 m² (60ft²)

Guttering
1 x 6 m (20ft) PVC or fiber cement gutter with round channel
1 x 2.3 m (7 ft 6 in) PVC or fiber-cement downpipe
1 gutter outlet
5 gutter brackets
2 stop ends
2 downpipe brackets
1 downpipe shoe
clout nails or screws

Fasteners
clout nails, roofing screws and hoop iron

Floor
1,800 kg (3,970 lb) cement
2.7 m³ (95 ft³) sand
4 m³ (140 ft³) stone

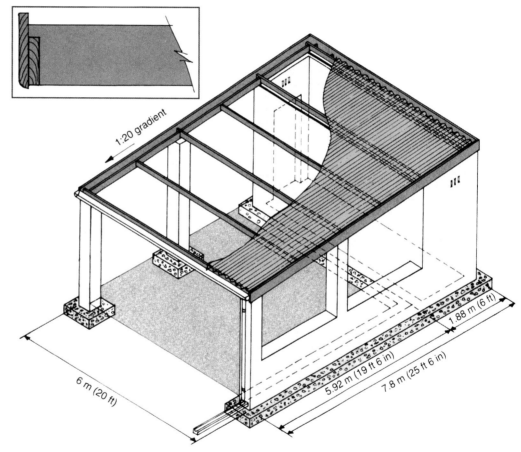

1. Dig two pillar foundations, 700 mm x 700 mm x 250 mm (2ft 4 in x 2 ft 4 in x 10 in). Dig strip foundations (if needed for your design, otherwise 4 pillar foundations) for walls, 700 mm (2ft 4 in) wide and 250 mm (10 in) deep, length as indicated.

2. Place concrete into the foundations and cast the slab; allow to set for 24 to 48 hours.

3. Build the pillars to a height of about 2.4 m (8 ft), reinforcing with rods from foundation level. Build hoop iron into last five courses.

4. Build the retaining wall and shed according to plan with hoop iron at corners of shed. Front pillars should be slightly lower than the back wall of the shed to allow for drainage. Construct outside walls with a cavity and build in airbricks directly opposite each other. Allow mortar to set thoroughly before assembling roof structure.

5. Fix beams in place with hoop iron. Saw out notches 50 mm (2 in) wide and 228 mm (9 in) deep at ends of purlins and slot into position at equal intervals along the structure (see detail sketch). Nail down.

6. Nail fascia boards to three sides of the structure.

7. Fix corrugated iron sheeting to beams over carport; alternate iron and fiberglass sheeting over shed.

8. Attach gutter and downpipe to the beam at the front of the structure.

More Carport Ideas

ABOVE RIGHT
Precast pillars and an aluminum sheet roof are the basis for this striking carport. Striped shadecloth has been added on one side to give added protection from the wind and rain. Different colored cement paving bricks have been laid to form a pattern on the driveway and parking surface.

CENTER
South American bougainvillea has been allowed to cover this wooden carport framework to give shade in sunny and hot weather.

RIGHT
A sturdy double carport built with wood has a corrugated metal roof.

TOP
Located in an urban area where space is limited, this carport not only provides shelter for cars, but also protects people entering the house.

ABOVE LEFT
Neatly tucked away, this carport with its green glass fibre sheeting roof has been built in front of the garage.

LOWER CENTER LEFT
Shadeports are becoming increasingly popular and there is now a large range of colors to choose from. Here a paler shade of gray was chosen to match the color of the roof tiles.

LEFT
Shadeports are lightweight and therefore effective when it is necessary to span a double driveway without the need for large footings and uprights.

INDEX

Made in the USA
Coppell, TX
06 September 2020

36133880R00040